The
LAST BOOK
of
WISDOM

PASTOR JAMES OKON

authorHOUSE®

AuthorHouse™
1663 Liberty Drive
Bloomington, IN 47403
www.authorhouse.com
Phone: 1 (800) 839-8640

Published by AuthorHouse 03/12/2019

ISBN: 978-1-7283-0409-0 (sc)
ISBN: 978-1-7283-0408-3 (e)

Library of Congress Control Number: 2019903000

CONTENTS

INTRODUCTION

Welcome to the wisdom of the age, the bedrock of sound procession. You are about to ponder on the entries of James Harvest, dragged from the quiet cave to the curious page. The volumes are great, but you have an opportunity of being an active participant in the art of elucidating the workings of the world around you as you go through so much of this volume that has been narrowed into principles. Principles indeed they are, and not stories. This is why you need the mother of all virtues, humility, to really understand how they work for you.

The wisdom in these entries does not just speak to your head, it speaks to your heart; revealing deep and secret thing about you and the world around you to you in order for you to make informed decisions about life and living.

I am conscious of the variations in the constitution of our different consciousness or probably, our consciences, based on the way our societies/ environments have shaped us. But the basic principles of life apply, and do not change, the more reason I find them more beneficial to you than stories. Fiction is good for the entertainment, but principles make you in life. Principles are not cast on cement but take the form of a point light, shining in all directions, whichever beam strikes you. You also have the opportunity to choose your own way of understanding the way these principles apply in your life, and the many questions they can help you answer without batting an eyelid, and these are questions that bug your peace times and confront you in daylight.

There are a few things you have to hold close and dear as you go through the pages, to be able to gain the best of the art in print;

First, you will find James, as a character and recipient, mentioned here and there in the book. You have to assume his position in order to perfectly position yourself as a second person in the communication of facts.

You will need to read between the lines, a few entries at a time —one is enough for a day — spending the rest of the time to ponder what they may possibly mean to you. After you find what it means to you, find conversant terms and put it in your own way in your mind.

Principles are almost useless outside their own settings, just like locks and keys, they only fit their own. But you have to keep them in mind, even at your fingertips, so that you are not taken unawares by circumstances. You may need at least one failure in their applications to integrate them in your wealth of experience. But please, do not cram.

The entries take the masculine in the second person. This should be understood to be due to the first recipient, but principles are what they are, applying to the both sexes.

Some facts of life are emboldened to give easier and quicker access to at least ten facts in an entry, but they do not represent thousands of other facts abundant in each entry.

Observing these things, you are now set for the adventure. Go out to a quiet place; you can take a trip to an island, where there is peace and tranquility. Develop some curiosity, or create a vague picture of your ignorance. Accept the challenges that they pose and go in with a purpose. Your major aim should be to find answers to life questions. Do not make an entry and come out without something to bless your curious mind. Share your findings with a close friend. You can say a lot, directing a mind to an entry.

The principles of life are the prophecies of the future; when you follow a particular road, you are sure to end where the road is leading.

There are 250 entries in the medley package. It is not the idea of the writer to arrange them into sections, but simply letting the ideas flow, from the crucial to the more essential, just the way they were handed down to me. They are all built for you, though they cannot all apply at the same time.

Wisdom is proven by the result it produces in the lives of those who follow after it.

Enjoy your voyage.

TO MY SON JAMES

1

WISDOM

I have watched you go about in silent talks and moody smiles. I have wondered what will become of your dissimilative life. The most interesting is when I watch you talk to yourself. I have come to realize the wisdom in you and how empty of it you feel. You must know that the first step to wisdom is the awareness of ignorance. **Seeking the knowledge of things from the source of truth is the right path, follow it!**

There is a height you want to attain and it starts from where you stand. Do not bother so much that you do not know me, but be console that I know and love who you are. Do not be afraid I call you my son for certainly your Father is in heaven and your biological father lives on. When you walk on the streets, do not stop and turn around trying to know who I really am and from where I watch, for you will only displease yourself.

I inquired your worse of fears but was stunned when you replied that you are afraid you are not as wise as you ought to be.

Do not ignore the advice of one who knows better than you do in any matter, especially when such has your good interest at heart.

Wisdom flows into the head with the breathe of air, and age is a cost.

Wisdom is not a product of the length of days, but of the best you make the use of the few, the days you live. Do not make yourself a specimen for life experiments, be quick to learn from the experiences of others. There have been old fools ruled by wise kings in their morning hours, and so far, the city of Athenia has produced the highest number of fools history has bothered to report.

Do not ever tell anybody you are wise for a single wisdom has a thousand and one foolish ends you would be surprise. My biggest mistakes in life often come from my 'wise' decisions.

Do not let knowledge fool you, you never know a thing until you have known the whole, and it is wisdom to know the whole truth of a matter before you make a statement.

Much learning does not bring understanding if the heart is not applied to wisdom. Your approach to a matter determines what you will find, a man who comes from behind can never know the mind.

Beware of prejudice! If your heart can not handle your preconceived opinion of life, do not come any further, my cave is beyond your bounds.

Do not be a defender of the truth except the whole truth you know, for many defenders of the faith have ended up killing and persecuting the true faithful.

The heights of great men reached and kept were not attained by a sudden flight. Yes, this is one of the things I learnt in school. Great men balance their tears with cheers and their smiles with frowns. They work in the plays of friends and toil in the hours of sleep.

You will never fill unless you realize your emptiness

and a full glass of water cannot accommodate an additional drop.

Let us Just be friends in black and white, thus, in pen and paper to be precise.

You have chosen the right path seeking to manage the affairs of your life with frictions that can never erode. You are of the special breed, of the few who tow the path of wisdom.

Even if you were not born to be a star, you will end up as one if you keep heading towards the sky.

Let every fear be brought to the slaughter and anxieties delivered to Hades.

2

SUCCESS

I appreciate your fears about the ends of human affairs. Many people you mentioned met unfortunate ends not because they had face-offs with fortune. They labored many enough but did not observe one thing that I wish you observe from today.

In whatever you do and are, always look forward to the end; success is not what you have, but what you have become.

Yesterday's future is today's realities. Do not talk about tomorrow with too much mystery, like a day that will never come; for before yesterday was over, tomorrow was already here. You thought it will never happen to you, but here you are buried right in it. The miracles you expected never happened; the sweet things have turned sour because you never bothered to look deeper. The tiny errors you allowed have ended up as monumental shame.

Living for the moment is a sweet sensation, but the moment does not make the life, it goes beyond.

When you straighten the paths in your school, you find out that you cannot make a straight path unless the man at this end looks forward to the other end of the road.

This is how it is in life, the end it is said, justifies the means.

On whatever courses you undertake, look forward to the end and be sure it is in line with what you want.

If anything is at variance, try some change,

and the best time for change is when you are not far into it.

If you are already far into it, you have a chance to start afresh being happy that you never met the end you never desired. Also, at whatever stage you are, judge yourself as if you are in a court of no appeal.

An unexamined life it is said is not worth living at all.

You may be surprise why I had to bring no appeal into the court and argue such does not apply.

It does not apply to us but it applies to you.

From yourself you can hide nothing and your conscience you cannot bribe. If you seek appeal from yourself, who will you go to? Nobody can judge you better than you judge yourself and you can tell no other truth than you know in yourself. It is only a faith fool who is committed to nonsense.

Faith in life is your commitment, not these arguments. The farthest way to success in life is the way of arguments; it never gets anything done and drowns its ship.

Do not fall into the trap of self-deception, that some spirits will make straight your crookedness without your positive effort. Luck does not exist in life, it is created by men who are diligent in their way and their work. If God had wanted to do it by himself, He would not have appointed you unto it.

Be careful how you believe what you do not understand!

The best friends that ever exist do not know a good part one of the other person. The people that help you in the wrong today will be the very people who will use the wrong against you tomorrow.

One more condition James,

Let the judgment add a little more joy to your soul and present to you a vision of your prize.

The first test of character is the zeal to discover self. The second test is what you do with what you have. Knowledge without action will end up as nonsense. Vision without concurrent mission won't build a kingdom.

Do not conclude that you are poor and be content with.

The identity of a poor man who will end up in great riches is that he will search and discover why he is poor, and then he will spend the rest of his life to destroy the cause of his poverty.

> *A man who cannot at least discover the cause of his poverty is not worthy of any riches.*

How would you feel if halfway you realized you had fallen out of track? Your strength is bound to down and your grimace find a light-out expression. If halfway you find you are in consonant with your end, it will double your strength and replace frowns with smiles.

This is why you should even

> *be more careful the way you start in life. A porous foundation if built upon can collapse the best of designs.*

Is there anything in your life you know so well you can't be wrong? What would you do if you were to realize you were wrong all along? It does not matter how certain you think you are of what you do or say, you can possibly be wrong.

> *If you cannot leave within your right a room for the possibility of error on your part, then you are too weak in character to be given serious consideration.*

So many people have said before that some things cannot be done only to wake up the very next day to find somebody do it. If you can explain what cannot be done, right in that exigesis is the root of solution.

3

GRATITUDE

Concerning the sense of gratitude you wished to know, it is a reaction to action if you would not mind. Every action that is not reacted to keeps the mind depressed of external thrust. Human ingratitude does not find its expression towards the creator alone, but applies too to the fellow man.

> *Gratitude is human bound to the all caring Creator.*
> *He who neither increases nor decreases in status nor strength,*

He who is enthroned by the praises of our lips. No man is bound by gratitude except one that has realized God has done something to him or his person.

Man must learn to be grateful not only for the things we asked and received, but also for those things we asked, but were not given to us by the wisdom of God, for do we consider what our lives would have been like, if those foolish requests of ours were granted yesterday, the opportunities we would be missing today, what our whole life would be like? So many people who enjoy life and prosperity today, had at some point in their life wished to die.

When some men cry, angels burst into laughter, because they know that had it been that the eyes of men are open to see what God has done for us in allowing some things to happen, we would be the happiest people on earth and not go about with sorry looks. After those years of tears and swearing, I thank God today that I did not marry her even though I loved her, imagine what I would be facing today.

God is and He is and cannot be and seize to be.
Gratitude keeps the flow and ingratitude breaks the bonds.

Little things build mounts of care

and create memories evergreen.

When you have gone higher upon the ladder of life in learning and wisdom, knowing the things that you should know, then you will come to discover amazing wisdom in little things, the intangible benefits and awesome powers embedded in the free gifts of nature.

I recall the game we used to play in school, rolling the ball one to the other. The game will never continue unless the one appreciate the gesture of the other throwing the ball in his direction and decides to do the same. You may wonder what we earned at the end but this is how we had happiness to our gain without the game depreciating in its value.

Every human and being has a warehouse of affection and gifts

you may be surprised. You may find the truth in this if you study the wicked man in your town, he is even in love with someone and bearing gifts; you can imagine the havocs that have been wreaked in this world to protect loved ones, how many wars have been fought and millions died for the love of one.

In this game of exchange, you either maintain the key to the warehouse with gratitude or close the door against yourself with ingratitude. You may choose to lose to gain or gain to lose.

Do not wait until you receive for none will come your way.

The first to give is the hero of the game.

4

WORLD PEACE

The world needs peace and it is capable of receiving that. Who can give peace to the world is not without the world but within.

Outside man, other creatures will be happier if there were more whims of disorder. Man is the only animal that needs peace and the only that can give it. I cannot give you peace and you cannot give me but we can give ourselves the best of the peace we need.

> *Peace is the discipline in bringing the elements of disorder*
> *to accept the terms of order.*

To do this the best, you need the discipline in the art of persuasion. The glory of your art lies in the conquer of yourself.

> *The best of men, who can bring others to peace, is he who is*
> *at peace with himself.*

Man is so blessed that he is blessed with reasoning abilities, something he has gotten more than any other animal under the face of the sun.

The solution to world crisis lies within these abilities: if you think before you act, and I reason before I react, then, and only then will we have peace in the world.

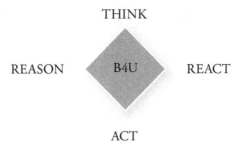

All the crisis in the world is only a question of simple understanding, especially when those who know nothing want to say everything moving their faith fools into action; when error is taught in the name of religion.

How else can you explain that we say the same thing and are fighting at the same time?

If you think you know the truth, be careful, lest you be put to shame when the beam is shone a little brighter. It begins with you; there is always that one man! The greatest opposition to light is the dark. It is much easier to give more light than to bring a tiny light to those in complete dark. When you see religion and the things that pertain to God being brought into argument, there you see men who are ignorant. God is not logical, He is revelational!

Your person is an entity with the arms of decisions, scrutiny and enforcement. Make some harmony between these arms and come out of yourself.

How many policies did you make within yourself and how many were you able to enforce. If the various members were not convinced by the persuasion in your terms of decision and cooperated accordingly realizing it was for the good of the whole body, how many would you have been able to enforce? Now take your place in the world as a significant part of it and member of its body. Do to the world the same thing you expected the members of your body to do to you. If you can forgive your teeth for biting your tongue, how come you find it difficult to forgive your husband or wife for her mistakes?

If only you be at peace with yourself, the world will be at peace with itself.

We can apply Dalton's principles termed. The law of partial pressure here by replacing pressure with peace. The total amount of peace in a medium (our world) is the sum total of the individual peace of its component members (me and you).

5

PEACE II

Concerning your argument about peace and endurance,

endurance brings peace to man.

Members of the body are different, one from the other. Different things in a donkey years act but once in the same way.

Members of the body cannot and should not be identical devoid of variation as this will only make them a group and deprive them of a body.

Peace only starts to reign when the individual members realize the difference that exists in the other.

It does not stop here, but when we have the knowledge of this difference, we have to complement it with the ways of managing these differences in other to compromise between antagon and tandem. This compromise will not present the mind with an ideal tandemism nor wildest antagonism but a synchrony of both.

You cannot experience the peace that there is if you fix your mind on the storm; look away from the storm around you and you can there and then experience the peace and serenity that there is.

We all seek in our daily lives to present ourselves some perfect models for some course, our wives, husbands, employer or career.

Even though there is no perfect man, every man is capable of attaining perfection in his chosen endeavor.

If iron must be beaten into shape, then it must endure the heat and the blacksmiths hammer.

No man can be perfected without these trials, and no trial will announce its coming or the form of its taking. A man who cannot bear to fit will remain a misfit.

A man is born worthy of nothing, but by training, we have become kings, lords and princes. There is no royal blood, the secret is the training. And with a good training, any man can excel in life and destiny.

When a man has allowed himself to be perfected for the course of his life, then his peace begins.

A man must first be at peace with himself, then in extension, be at peace with others.

My tutor in the music discipline taught me that

> *harmony is a better part of music than solo. A one man band is easy, but more beautiful when two can work together in unity.*

The knowledge of endurance is the acquisition of peace.

> *The enduring is the master of himself and the Lord of humanity.*

You find people ask the other to control one's self when he/she gets angry. It then follows that whoever is able to make you angry controls you.

How many people would like that others or things without them have the control of their lives?

The greatest war, it is said, is the war with ourselves.

If you then can control yourself, you are a worthy model for every fellow human.

Endurance is strength that cannot be beaten by strength.

> *What makes other human beings scream will only tickle an enduring person to laughter.*

Have you ever read or heard of the Spartan boy? Our teacher used to tell us this story when we were children.

An enduring person will live with any man but a man devoid of endurance will never cope with the best of gods.

6

FOOD

When I was a little boy, my father used to watch me eating. He will quickly ask what the problem is if we never smiled to show we are happy.

Sadness brings distaste to food and food reduces the intensity of grieve.

When I was angry as a child, as many children often do, the first reaction in my mind was to refuse participation on the table. I always wondered what benefit I will derive being an unhappy participant on a table of blissful minds.

To me,

> *it was better an empty table than that filled with food eaten without joy.*

We know where happiness comes from, that the things we want happen to us the way that pleases us. But this joy, so needed but not found, with so much money to buy but no merchant to sell except one who doesn't trade on bags of gold.

> *It is strange the things that God gives to the poor, that they can marry for love and dance in streams of joy.*

Food is more than a supply of chemical energy, but an occasion for emotional construction.

People finish a cow but grow thinner while others go with a piece but grow fat. It is all the work of their emotional disposition.

Whatever gives the faint of emotion either within or without meals should properly be settled before meals.

When you sit on the table for meals, make sure you discuss the issues of the heart; this hunger is stronger than bread and wine.

Many people go with feeble limbs and protruded stomach synonymous to patients of severe pellagra, but they have on their tables better meals that should ensure a difference.

An unhappy person can poison himself with the best of continental dishes not because any poisonous substance has been included, but because he / she enters to a poisonous limit trying to overcome his mental position. While many happy people take a glass of wine to increase their emotional excitements and be healthier looking, the unhappy ones are busy with gallons of ethanol to gab the bridge of impulse transfer in their brain. For how many minutes will the break of impulse and depression continue? How long will you continue this way?

Joy is the value of meals and food should be received with thanks.

Joy is about the only supplement needed for a healthy soul, and the outward manifestation depicts the state of the soul.

Joy is the free gift of God to a contented soul.

Joy is the sunshine of the soul; it brings the light that recreates the being, redeeming all that have otherwise been battered by life.

The volume of food is no determining factor in health but the quality which is highly determined by your emotional disposition.

There are many hungers more important than food on the table.

Food, in fact, should be the last part of meals.

7

EXPECTATIONS

Human emotions are not steady but maintained.

The rise and fall of emotions are ruled by expectations.

Excitements set the upward movement while depression sets the downward trend of emotions.

Excitement and depression should be expected one in place of the other when there has not been established a trust.

It is better to launch a man a surprise than delay a promise.

Surprises send emotions to their potential point kilometers above the maintained position. This is to say

surprises come millions of hours ahead of the expected time.

This is how we raise the spirit of man and increase his span of life.

At the expected time, emotions come down to the maintained position. Beyond this point, human emotions are eroded at the rate of 60 minutes per hour.

Human expectations have their values of excitements attached base on dignity.

When the dignity of a thing has been completely eroded, receipt of such takes-off some dignity from the recipient to balance the difference. Surprises add to the dignity of the giver to raise him/her to the position of his/her gift.

Surprise visits make the soul overflow.

How would you feel if you were suddenly smiled upon by the beam of fate? How would you feel if it were a frown?

Fate is the goddess of luck and luck is an ambivalent term. I hate the two of them but am certain they will come one at its time.

I do not hate them because they come but because they make me feel I am not in control of my life or that some forces without controls my within.

Delays milk the soul of fantasy and send emotions yonder.

The best players in the game of gifts are those who expect surprises and delays at every time.

Unforeseen circumstances are one virus that plagues the corporations in my state, I do not know if it is the same with you.

Even when uncertainty abounds, you need to create some certainty to advance.

Even this was what it used to be before the grand corruption of an age that has labored so hard to strip itself of morality; the only certainty you can have is that you are uncertain of what will be the outcome.

Any man who depends on the promises of men these days will a thousand times be broken in pieces; for if you depend on my promise which depends on a promise that depends on a promise, you cannot justify the blame when I am a victim of a failed promise too.

I can even tell you of collaterals that entitles you to nothing, even of a thousand engagements that translates into a thousand broken relationships, no marriage, even a thousand marriages no wedding.

It is only fools that speed ahead when they cannot even see their way and they crash somewhere anyway.

In a society where there is neither trust nor confidence, human sufferings is bound to multiply.

Do not play with the mind and do not drain desires.

It is better done earlier.

8

HYPOCRISY

It is in the character of every sane man to hate what is dirty. Many people do not realize what is dirty and others refuse to accept the fact of dirtiness in dirty things and scenes. What is dirty is repulsive but not all repulsive things are dirty.

Due to variations in human character affected by the environment of development, things dirty in my judgment may not apply to your scrutiny. Finding a universal definition of terms have become the business of many professions, an attempt to communicate facts across experiences with unitary comprehension.

There is one vain dissipation I have observed in human piety and that is dragging clean things to dirty places. There is a trend in the religious society, that men get themselves into a mess, then try to drag God into it.

If anybody hates what is dirty, it's the Spirit of the Most High.

I have seen bloodstained hands raising to the heavens and accursed lips reading the words of benediction. I have seen words of blessing on the tombs of wicked men, and I ask why? Even when the dead cannot bite? I have seen wayward women saying there are no husbands, and when I looked again at them, I can't find a wife.

Clean houses attract clean men while dirty ones harbor filths. Clean thoughts proceed form clean minds while dirty hearts get the lips to babble evil. When you keep your house clean, clean people will come to dwell.

> *The spirit of the most high will not enter a dirty place even on invitation.*

When I see evil men prophesy of holy scenes,

I wonder if I deceive them or they think they deceive me.

If I have never read the word of God before, I would wonder if He ever talks at all. It is as if each time God does not respond according to human timing, one crafty man will wake up and speak on His behalf what he would have expected Him to say.

And the more people are willing to obey the word of God, the more deceivers appear who use His name to fleece. The more God hides His face from men, the more humans create toys to represent Him. Maybe God should just appear to everybody anyway, that way men would know when demon possessed men are lying about God; but we have His Word!

When men perpetrated wickedness in the name of customs and tradition, the people appealed unto religion to save the day, but what do you see in religion?

A preacher that does not practice what he preaches; a follower that is only by the name. An abomination that has translated into a tradition, now it is even a religion. How much many men wish their way should be the true way, so they would not bother to loose their comfort to change; and then they turn around and deny there is a true way causing men to queue behind their error. And when a man can invest sufficient words, a religion can be created out of every thought pattern.

If a holy God should speak through evil lips, then He is not fit to be my true God.

It is a big mistake in this age to believe the things you hear, and whoever receives a prophet for what he is called will receive a deceiver's reward.

You must take people by what they do and only a very little of the volumes they speak.

There are many gods you must understand, and when a man claims to be speaking and acting in God's name, it is good to ask which of the gods. And if you have a God who does not talk to you, ask Him why? Every other god is talking, even of nonsense.

Clean people will never mind helping dirty ones to become clean.

Clean pretenders abound and I will not wish you are any of them. These ones will never be clean because they do not know they are dirty.

The Almighty One has kept everything in place to assist you to be clean and he will come to rest.

You only need to co and he will operate.

For one thing I know of him, he has never paid an empty visit. He will not leave your heart without leaving behind a sign.

9

BELIEVE

I know how much you are afraid of a believe but you must believe in something; being or person.

Many who scout for the best die on the way.

It would be better not to believe anything at all considering how many have been disappointed by the things they believed, but this is not the best part of human life.

Though confusion has become the order of the world, you do not need to be confused. So many people are searching for things in life without finding, but the law of God states that if you search, then you will find. Sometimes, right in the place people said something does not exist is where others will come to find the same thing.

If you do not belief that something is there, you might not be able to find it; but the man who believes that it is there will keep searching until he finds it.

You have to be protected by what you believe and this has nothing to do with weapons or armor. The feeling of protection is an emotional state that must be triggered by the contemplation on the potentials of your believe. If after due consideration you do not still feel protected, it is one sign you have no believe or have believed on what you should not believe. I will not believe in God who is known to protect those who believe in Him and still go around with a loaded gun.

> *One day you will come to understand that a man is nothing without God, except he that can defend himself effectively in the spirit world.*

Protection is not the only, you also have to be rich.

Riches has not necessarily to do with wealth but a sense of contention. If you can feel protected and rich, it is one sign you have a believe but you need to be happy.

You may argue any person that is rich and protected should be happy but the mind is almost always divided on this. If with riches and protection you are not happy, it is a sign that you had done something indecent to forge this state of mind, check yourself.

You have known that there are gods; but you must also know that there is God. The gods will never do for man what God has not permitted to be done or beyond the powers allowed them by God.

Let wisdom guide you that you do not work for the very enemy you are trying to fight against.

Above all, you need to be satisfied. Satisfaction does not come in quantity or quality but emotional disposition to the prevailing situation.

You never know how useful money can be until you come into lack, nor how useless it can be until you have a large bank account.

Neither the poor or the rich is ever satisfied as long as his eyes are on money.

Anybody that has no vast mass should have a strong root in other to survive.

The wind of confusion of this life will never carry a vast mass or uproot a strong root but any less is a victim. This is why we see poor people go into piety and the rich into festivity.

In the two cases what comes into play is believe.

The rich believes in the mass of his wealth while the poor in the strength of his God.

He that is not protected, rich, happy and satisfied in what he believes, has no believe. Religiously he has no mass nor roots and thus a victim of the wind.

10

FRIENDSHIP

Friendship is a necessary part of life. No matter how much you want to be my friend, you may not need to be my friend. You must know the thing that brings you to me, and be sure it is what I can always give, for thus far can our friendship last. Many people seek to take advantage of friendship than develop the vantage of friends. Many people seek to have miracles in life even in the places where they are supposed to be the miracle for others.

When things go well with you, you do not need to ask for friends; they will come.

> *As a drop of honey catches many flies, so a bag of money brings many friends.*

When things go bad, do not struggle too much to keep your friends, bear in mind that they will go.

The only unfortunate situation in this case is when all are gone and not a single one left.

> *If things do not go wrong, you may not really know who was your friend all along.*

Your worst enemy can be your best friend it is said, and your best friend can be your worst enemy. But it does not have to be you.

I have discovered one thing in life, that the fake is always shiny to enter the eye; and if you are not sure of what you are looking for, you are bound to fall for the fake ones. The best way to sell a fake is to give it an attractive package, the first step to successful prostitution is to at least dress to catch men's attention. When the eye has seen good, it does not take the mind much time to decide.

It follows that

> *whoever deserts you at your point of need, never needed you at your time of plenty.*

If people never feel your absence, they either never needed your presence, or your influence is so insignificant to be felt.

One of the worse mistakes you can do in friendship is to appeal to obligation. People do not like obligation, it is the more you give, the less you get, and if you want to keep your friends, you must be content with this.

If you are wise, you would allow your friends to take responsibility for their actions, and the more responsible your friends are the better for you.

In all these, do not seek so much that anybody will do your things for you, you have the sole responsibility towards yourself. In school we had friends for food and friends for good and each had their roles to play.

The fact that all your friends are gone does not imply you should not make friends again.

Old clothes wear, giving place to new ones. The first thing to expect in human relationships is disappointment.

Do not sit and wait for the disappointment to come, you have the duty of giving excitement.

> *Even if every other person should fail you, do not fail yourself.*

It is not finished until you accept the end. You are the worst that can disappoint yourself and so leave no stone unturned. But if you are the kind that banks on another man's account, you have already failed yourself, for it is the time that you need people the most, that is when they are sure to fail.

11

EMOTIONS

Concerning these love affairs, it is an office to make no mistakes but yet mistakes make the spice of love. If the eyes were to see all that there is, then there would be no love found among the sons of men.

Look good and smell good, these are the primary requirements for getting love, and if you are good, you will keep what you have gotten.

There are three windows to the mind; the eye, the ear and the nose. If you can get into the mind through one of these, then you will certainly get attention. And if you present a sweet promise, then you can court affection.

Emotional obsession gives rise to a gap of reason.

Infatuation is the necessary disease of love that is only cured by circumstances and time. Love qualifies the unknown and justifies without a proof. If love catches you like fever, time will cure it; if it burns in you like fire, then reality will quench it, if it throws you off balance, then the losses will teach you a lesson. If it is not a commitment then do not take the argument, do not explain.

We know time to be the greatest healer and revealer of secrets but what can we say of circumstances? "Don't worry", is one slang that prevails in courtship but it is more adhoc than official.

When you take don't worry home in a matter of serious concern, then you put your life in line for bitter regrets.

We all have got our parts to play in a love affair and each person's part is no less than the other's.

In the shadow of blindness love sees,

but the spell of infatuation blocks the strength of reaction. If you have the habit of reacting to every wrong, then you will die an old lonely fool.

Do not let your love do your own part of the love demands; it will make him loose some amount of faith.

The fact that he loves you cannot be denied but for how long is what you must guard. Seek the knowledge of your duty and do not allow him do the whole of the job. Duty kills affection by routine, give every circumstances due courtesy, give love what is desired per time.

The fact that he had agreed to be coming does not mean you should not be going or immediately he sets his eyes on one who agrees to be coming, your case needs no summary to be determined. Do not starve love, this way has killed many mighty and strong.

Lovers defend their investment, of time, energy and resources.

If she has nothing to lose, then you are facing a serious risk; and if you place too much burden of obligation from your care, then you may become a problem that needs an immediate solution.

You are not the most amazingly wonderful girl he has ever met in his life and you will not be, though he may say that to arouse your desire. Butterflies do not bury a fallen flower; they only fly to the next one standing with a promise of pleasure.

If his love has made him speak, let your desire make you act.

For you to act in the best ways, you have to tell yourself a little lie; that this is the first man, the last man and the only man you have ever met in your life. If you can thus deceive yourself, you are for sure the most wonderful in the historical books of love.

While he loads his own side of the love boat, load your own side, or you will sooner experience a capsize and you do not know who will survive.

12

GIVING

The whole business of living is about giving and receiving. One side of it is an obligation, and that is giving while the other is an accident, and that is receiving.

> *You may never reap unless you sow and can possibly not reap what you have sown.*

But in all these, a seed that you have not sown will never grow, you can never succeed in a venture you have not started, every positive effort in life is an opportunity taken.

> *A child that plants a tree in the morning will have enough shade to cover his head in the hot afternoon. If he saves his money to buy a blanket, he will escape the freezing cold of the winter nights. Over the years I have learnt, that tomorrow never tarries; before you close your eyes and open again, it is already here.*

You may have friends who come your way only because of what they can get from you, and it is a popular way of psyching a gal telling her of what she can get if only she falls your way. But when spreading your wings like the peacock, know that women now earn what they spend.

> *Do not let your faith be in what you can get but in what you can give in relationships.*

The only promise that delivers in a relationship is of what you want to give to it. Very many people are only interested in what they can get from a situation or person and very few think of what they can give.

> *The reason public officials set winds of confusion is only that they may gain from the crisis that may arise. If more money will be spent on the military when the state is fighting a war, then why will the military authorities not set up one for the state to fight?*
> *Any man that has received a better promise will find every occasion to dispense of the old covenant. When a man's heart is already set on another woman, then a broken cup can be enough reason to sue for a divorce.*

Disappointments come as a result of failure of expectations, but determination will always ensure eventful and active relationships.

Do not rely on yesterday's kindness for tomorrows favors, the last thing that men want to pay is debt, even the debt of gratitude.

If you are fooled to so think that because you were kind to a man yesterday, that he will do same to you today, better buy a rope, for you will soon hang yourself.

Do not expect the reward of your gesture from the recipient, for you were not created one for the other, but the return of your gift will come from someone you cannot repay.

When it comes to your mind that your friend has not given enough compared to what you gave, think also of how many people you owe the much they gave to you.

It follows that you should not even compare what you get to what you gave.

Givers never lack, it is often said, and lack never gives.

If you hold onto what you have, where will what you want come to stay?

Men do not give because they cannot keep back what they have, but simply because they understand the importance of giving in life.

> *Pass the game to the next player so that the better part of it may come to your position.*

The joy of giving alone is enough a good return to people who give.

Do not give so much to those who repay you nor go into friendship for the sake of what you can get.

Those who need your gifts make better friends for you for they owe you the debt you will never ask a repay. When men are cornered to pay back, then you can expect a show down.

13

DEATH

Death is a necessary end to life, the most precious thing we have. The epignosis of life exists in death, the truth that we live to die. We all die but not all live, even those who live, not all will die, and even all who die, they shall all live. It is life at the beginning and life at the end because the beginning and the end is life, even death is a life separated from life.

> *Death may have a scary look but it is the best of human friends.*

An example of human careless choices, a choice once made and cannot be changed, and yet changed to perfect purpose.

The ugly Oge said, "One thing I hate about man is, they hate me before they even get to know me".

This is true of man and death, we hate death before we even get to know it.

Nobody has had a kiss of death and resists its grip, yet we think it is awful, who has ever screamed? Man screams of fear and not of death and no man has ever seen death and scream of it. Death never hurts, it only soothes, the best friend that comes to a tired life.

> *He that appreciates not death has no complete knowledge of his dear life.*

Anxiety is not our best friend and will never be.

We have not yet seen but greater things and death is the greatest of them all. It is the only food we see and desert all, eat of it and never want.

It is obvious in fact, we will all die, for what would our world be if death had not been. Do those who seek protection from death live the full length of their lives?

> *Death meets the weak at tired age and the strong at their*
> *tender age.*

This is one simplicity that roams the domain of men, allowing ourselves to be tossed by our token of fear.

I have seen men sell themselves into slavery for fear of hardship but those who face the hard times will live free in the calm beyond.

We live to die an die to live but in all of these the truth is this; in whatever life we find ourselves we only have to do our best.

Death has kept his distance, encircling the life of man. You run away from this end only to meet the other end of death earlier than it should be.

To and fro movement does not profit a man and force without distance is a useless dissipation of energy.

When energy is gone, drought will come and drought will lead to a tired life. At the instance of a tired life, your humble friend death will come, with beams of smile to make your day.

> *The worst thing to befall a man is not death, but to live*
> *and die without fulfilling the very purpose for which you*
> *were born.*

There is no greater mercy the creator can bestow upon a man, than to give him enough time to finish what he has got to do in life.

Forget about what you leave behind, you can never tell what will befall them after you are gone.

14

REFLECTION

Life is not about shouts and lauds except for fools.

In little things we exclaim but all is vanity we agree.

We watch as big things become nothing, and even the things we always wanted to see, we find had to look. Imagine how yesterday's fashion has turned to rags, and how many people robbed, killed and maimed just to get one of these.

The pride of material possession is a symptom of lack of understanding; for every trash was once treasure and even in trash are buried priced possessions.

From cradle to grave is about desires and wants.

We are not satisfied by needs though they are more important to us. **The greatest frustrations in life have come from possessions, that we went so far to get a thing, only to find it altogether useless after all.**

Do not think your world is coming to an end when your nature blesses you with a little time to contemplate the past. What every man yearns for, a trouble free life is an illusion that only exist in utopia, but real life is full of challenges, just about how you handle them.

There is more wisdom in depression than in satisfaction.

Deep thoughts bring the soul closer to the body where they stay to communicate life prospects.

If what you have known is all you think you should know, then you are of all men, most miserable.

It is in the midst of crisis that is created great characters, the spinning of yarn yields precious linen, and turbulence turns milk to butter.

A state of satisfaction should be the worse that has ever happened to a man yet it is what we all must seek. Satisfactions exist much in the mouth because we do not want to displease.

There is more gain in meditation than in celebration.

Meditation sees defects while celebration is as blind as love.

Neither of meditation or celebration is inapt but by comparative advantage we talk of that which profits the mind, the very soul of man.

The sky is not enough for meditation while the roof top is a wonderful experience for celebration.

Meditation brings the past and the future to meet in the present, what then will not straighten?

The present is not enough and what you see is not more important than from where it came or to where it will go.

There is more fancy in passion than in fashion.

Following the whims of fashion has been the disease of seasons, when men and women enslave their reasons.

Every fashion will fade, but passion will stick to its model no matter what.

The zest for satisfaction leads men to depression, and in depression is revealed the neglected satisfaction.

Life is as sacred as it is contemplative, but festivities beef up our emotions.

There is death in both, the bitter and the sweet, only be sure you do not go too far either way; and in-between is the life of temperance.

It is all a matter of choice from wants, preferences to alternatives. You must as need be in life attain a right mental attitude before you can achieve the right altitude in life.

When through mental evolution you come to the awareness of self and the workings of your environs, then by knowledge you will gain the wisdom needed to scale the ladder of life to any altitude.

15

EMOTIONS II

Life is not all about love, it consists of hate. Both love from hate and hate from love meet and part to take their turns.

Love is intoxicating and it is what it was born to be.

There is nothing sweet about sweet, it is just that it is sweet and that is all.

Out of sound appraisal and careful consideration of the factors surrounding lovers, love would be locked in the cupboards.

> **Do not be overwhelmed by the number of people who love you, less you lose your sense of caution.**

Flowers were meant to attract birds and so is no extraordinary thing when they come.

Take away the nectar from the flower and birds will spit right in their face. It is one experience to be a beautiful girl in the Camp, you have a choice to cage or flirt.

It is good to know why they love you but the answer to this exists in old minds.

> **Perhaps many love you because they hate you and will never say it because they know this will scare you.**

Many still say they love you simply because they are not bold enough to say they hate you; after all love is an English word and any fool can pronounce it.

Some say what they do not mean and others do not mean what they say. But as a rule;

> *Do not be scared by the number of people that hate you, less you lose your feelings of passion.*

When I talk of hate I do not mean enmity.

Enmity is a form of human consciousness that is often unreal.

One man's meat may be another man's virus and a flower for one bird may represent a scarecrow for the other bird. **Some sadomasochists hate to see you happy, but this does not mean you should go sad to please their disease.**

You certainly do not need to cut your nose to spite your face. The only person you will come to appreciate most in the coming years will be the original you, and how it has endured the times. **Do not be confused about this, every fake is bound to fade some day.**

> *Both love and hate press on your sides to give you balanced step.*

This is one reason you do not need to be overwhelmed or scared, obsessed or depressed.

It is a virtuous office to maintain a level head with both those who love and hate you.

If you discard one, you will fall consequent of the other. If your friend or confidant does not betray you, your enemies will not overtake you.

Do not be quick to regret and do not run away; seek the knowledge of all things with all your means and this shall refine your perspective of life.

> *Knowledge my son is like the refiners fire; it will burn off stubbles, reveal hidden details and create great characters.*

The farther a place is, the nearer it is to some other place.

To run from hate is as good as falling prey of love.

Over consciousness of love is as delerative as the over-consciousness of hate.

16

RESPECT

Respect is a natural reciprocal of gesture. It is deserved and not purchased.

Respect comes with height of human achievement represented in personal easiness.

Respect is not coaxed from people and wise men do not seek them.

Respect is no alphabet in titles

for in my community, titles hang like giant robes on dwarfish thieves similar to the Shakespearean age.

Respect mongers like to be dressed in borrowed ropes and tigers by titles are scared by the croaking of frogs. Life is full of men who try so hard to maintain what they cannot defend, living the kind of life they cannot sustain.

Respectable and influential people humble themselves before their fellow men.

They have always humbled themselves because they learnt to humble themselves. Life is full of nobodies trying to be somebody by all means, be not carried away by men who claim to be everything with big titles and many claims.

Fools have no knowledge of their foolishness and this is what makes them fools in reality.

Fools are always proud of themselves, they know no atom of respect.

They will always be humbled because they have no atom of influence.

A positive impact will earn a man lasting influence, but fear will only earn him bitterness and disgust.

> *It is better to realize an insult than to seek respect from people.*

Respect yourself and who you are and the rest will be given to you. Even if the world around you should be filled with disrespect, you should give yourself enough respect.

> *A dumping site often begins with an empty can thrown in by the owner, then others follow suit.*

Even if you put a sign forbidding the act, if men see you do it, they will follow suit.

Do not bother yourself to go seeking for respect for you will only displease yourself but respect every single person as much as you can but not necessarily as they deserve.

It is one sad experience to climb a hill to be seen only to discover at the top that nobody is looking at you.

> *The throne is one position of respect that earns no respect from the ruled except for fear.*

While you are out to instill fear, have in mind that every deliberate attempt is open to challenge, but fear in itself is no sign of respect.

17

AMBITION

Life is all about struggle to attend the highest height of human endeavor. With the top, a visible horizon, we may ask why we cannot just wake and walk to it.

You need to struggle because you are not the only person with the vision of the height, but must be the first to attend it.

Some say the world would have been a better place if people didn't have to eat, if the mind was dead to desire and the heart satisfied.

> *But life loses its essence and purpose the moment there is nothing left to fight for or to conquer.*

A still birth is better than a life without purpose or ambition.

It is a matter of belligerence contending with forces within and without yourself in militia against the realization of your wildest dream.

> *Do not be discouraged in your struggle when you hear the suffering and pains that great men underwent.*

Nothing good comes in an easy way and the first to discourage you are the very people you had in mind.

Lock-up all fears and analyze all signals of solution.

There is no functional encyclopedia of solutions to the problems of life. Every problem is unique and requires a unique solution and the key is within the problem itself, how much you understand what you face.

Double your strength in the face of opposition and do not have faith in any person other than you.

Pains are like strikes that fall on a hot bent iron in other that it may straighten. Allow yourself to be obsessed by the joy of being recognized as a straight useful metal. If not for anything else, for the fear of being discarded, or turned into something worse than this. Those who do not succumb to be made fit for something only end up as good for nothing in life.

Sufferings are like intense heat and pressure that carbon accepts to be transformed into the precious diamond,

the hardest material humanity has ever known and for that a non-metal. You will never believe that diamond and graphite were twins of the same father Carbon. While diamond accepted the heat and pressure of training and is now found in palaces of exalted kings, graphite languished in pleasure and is today not fit even for common use.

You have no excuse not to attain whatever height you want in life, but as a price, you have to develop the capacity to contain the heat and pressure that will come from within and without in other to mold you to the best form.

Be inspired by the lofty heights of great men and let the attainment of it be your aspiration.

You have to understand that nothing precious comes out of nature without pressure.

Even the liquid gold, petroleum, would not have been without a long time of heat and intense pressure.

Inspiration is a wildfire that burns in human minds, ignited by reason

and raises the human mental temperature to the level that excites emotions and consequently set in a chain of physical reactions.

Those who do not want to suffer prefer to slope to the bottom of the mount.

It is these people who follow the path of least resistance that often end up amounting to nothing.

There is much to desire at the top than the things below your strength.

Of a truth, the higher you go, the tougher it gets, but the cooler it becomes. There is so much for the few people above, and so little for the many people below.

Do not trust the level you find yourself for nothing in life stays constant. It is either you advance or you are advanced.

But one thing is sure;

those who suffer to climb to the top of the mount of their dreams will experience the chilling sensation of the ice-cap.

Even if you die there, I promise you will never rot; even if you die, you will still live forever.

18

RELATIONSHIP

Life has got in stock series of responsibilities, and responsibilities entail action. To enhance the society, we go into associations of people and make friends as much as we can. At least one of the friendships we make often grow up to intimate levels that may careless of carnality.

In the intimate state of our friendships, we often exchange confidential that relieve our minds of some of the troubles that we encounter in life without leaving us with the trouble of protecting the confidence we have for each other. These intimate friendships are often realized by other members of the association who grow jealous consciously or unconsciously. In this state, we often are selected to keep custody of the moral and discipline of the association. Here you have a task that you have to succeed but not without influences that press on you from both sides. You have your friend and confidence to protect but not without the eyes and comments of your associates to avoid. What do you do?

In your actions, do not mix influence.

Your friends often go wrong because with you they feel relaxed, not without the eyes of others keeping watch over them.

In this, have a straight focus on the task and ignore the influence that may be. Let discipline be administered to whoever deserves and

do not give your friends unnecessary defense.

If governance was based on sound principles and not confraternity of few politicians, then the society would have seen justice and development.

For as long as politics is a game of interest, and these interest revolves around the public treasury, then the society is in danger of decay.

> *To withhold your hand from the good that you can do is as bad as doing evil itself.*

It is either you please one or you never act, or you may prefer to act and fail.

Be happy if you can please the both sides; this can only happen when you take out extra time to explain to your friend your position with respect to standards.

Your friends will rectify their position when they realize you would not dilute the rules to suit their frailty in all the actions that you must enforce; you can deprive yourself as much as you can, but never for once displease yourself.

There are no secrets between true friends except the ones they desperately try to keep about their own selves.

19

FAITH

It is hard to have faith in our world of today but life without faith is in deep confusion.

Faith establishes the direction of work

and work is a justification of the large joules of energy dissipated in life. Work without result is a waste, and too much of it will ruin your world.

For faith to be strong on that which is yet to be seen, then there must be an evidence of that which came into being.

A worker sees not his wages, but believes it will come, but when the first fails, what is the prove the second won't be the same.

Faith is a dimensional act intercepted by works throughout its stretch.

When faith is stretched into infinity without a tangible intermittent benefit; then search for deception.

Faith without work is useless says Saint James. Faith establishes calm in a person's life but infidelity is a potential of catastrophe.

Not work nor the reward for work has a defined magnitude or interval but is finally balanced proportional to the determinant of the substance:

Faith works for no reward but reward is the stem of faith.

Faith is a long term enterprise of human living.

Faith is not given but it is accepted, it is not sold but is purchased with works.

Faith is what we build and maintain, securing our hope of security.

Throughout history, of the times of kingdoms and nations and even in the present: more heinous crimes and evils have been perpetrated in the name of obedience to some authority than in rebellion, even in religion, where the supremacy and infallibility of the authority must not be questioned. There is little then left to wonder, if any authority that is not obeyed, can thus exist?

> *If God was to listen to the advice of men, I would prevail upon Him to defend Himself against those who perpetrate lies in His name.*

How would you feel realizing you are a god to your God and a king to your King? Surprised! Yet this is what you are; a faith to your faith, hope to your hope, a god to your God, a security to your agent of security and

> *by your existence, you establish the existence of your source of existence.*

Without a kingdom, there will never be a king. Every king has his domain, and God is overall. This is one secret in life you must keep in mind.

The only powerful man I know in this world is that man who enjoys the mercy and help of God, the rest is an empty claim.

A King is not more important than the subject and an object of faith is not more important than the faithful.

Disappointment is the virus of faith and the ability to deactivate it instills immunity against future occurrence.

How do you feel destroying that which your hands had built?

You may argue that this kind of things happen when we grow angry but do not forget that whoever and whatever succeeds to make you angry has control over your emotions. How about this;

> *Whoever breaks the faith he had built may never build a faith he can keep. If you always have a reason to change*

your convictions, you will always find a reason to change your faith.

A genuine faith will bring you three important things: light that cannot be quenched, life that cannot be destroyed, and power that cannot be conquered.

20

WISDOM II

Seek as much as you can the ability to judge the things of this life in their correct order and proportion. Try and realize the unimportant things as well as the important.

Learn which of your encounters has to be tasted, that to be swallowed as well as that which has to be chewed and digested.

The greatest thing that a man has need of in life is wisdom.

Wisdom is the principal thing in life, and above all is the gift of understanding.

It is wisdom that acquires knowledge and wisdom it is that puts the knowledge thus acquired into beneficial act.

But without understanding, knowledge is useless to any man. However true this may be, many human persons prefer tricks and sidelines.

Wisdom handles the affairs of his life with aptitude and ease of mind.

It is wisdom to learn from the past and visualize the future real and clear. It is wisdom to acquire the knowledge of things. In whatever you do, seek and know where you are, what you want, the ways you can get it, the way that suits you the best, your strength to get it, the ways you can develop upon it and with little but no time you have it with ease.

Knowledge defines the action of sane minds.

The things you do and the way you do them has much to tell about the knowledge that exists in you.

Ignorance is synonymous to disease but is not an excuse for inapt.

Actions that are not defined are dispersed and cannot establish a body of fact, and can be thought to come from minds that are insane.

Experience, people say, is the best teacher, while

intuition is the glory of imagination;

But in all these, creativity is the best part of human development. I have found out in life that specimens and experimental tools always end up destroyed, so I count it wisdom to learn from the experiences of others.

Defined action is the character of greatness. How would you feel realizing you are acting at the best times and known as a just judge?

Many people find it difficult to look beyond their actions less they would realize there is a deeper way than these.

Do not be scared of the discontentment that comes from personal failings, it is one of the things you need to go beyond your personal limitations.

Evils are done on very flimsy excuses and trivial reasons. Ask many felons why they committed havoc, you easily hear things as unwittingly as ignorance of consequence and revenge.

21

TRUE STRENGHT

I have by now had much delight watching the business of my friends that I feel I should bring to you a fair share of the things I have learnt from them.

My friend works in the steel mine and spends a good amount of his income and resource fashioning weapons.

The other works in cement quarry and spend days and nights heavy weight lifting. I have another friend who is a nuclear physicist who spends his time and energy fashioning dynamites.

I had a pretty good number of others with similar psychological orientation.

One day I called them to a party during which time I had an opportunity to hug and kiss my quests. Surprisingly, one had some dynamites in his pocket and the other a steel sword while the other had still a stainless gun and many others of the like, not forgetting those with shoulders of Atlas.

The party transformed into a meeting hall for psychological appraisal and they easily told me there were many others of their friends with the like mentality.

Does the soldier make the gun or the gun make the soldier? Does the fight cause the knife or the knife cause the fight? Are you sure you need a gun in case there is a war? Or you can start a war any time you like because you have a gun?

Or could it all have been avoided if the weapons were away, or would nations have gone to war if their amours never made them mad?

Did the war make the weapons or the weapons make the war? For every conventional weapon, there is a conventional war to fight. How

else where you going to test the weapon if you do not start a war that will see to its use?

Each one having his own armor to avoid being wounded by the others. None wants to die first nor give-up.

They so much trusted in their armor that at the slightest provocation will go to fight and prove their strength.

It seems to me that whenever a man sees in himself an advantage, he becomes mad to grab every opportunity.

These I realized are people who are controlled by the deeds of others devoid of control of their own emotions. I wondered how many of their breed have died for;

in every test of power, one must die or flee if witty and swift.

After thorough observation of them, I realized many things were special about me.

I had no scars on the head nor deformities and cuts on the body quite unlike many of them.

A man's future is secure within the permutations of his present choices.

I saw everybody as friends with wife and children and live in my own house quite unlike many of them. I saw myself at peace developing at a steady pace and a future quite assured. I had no blood on my hands, do not scream in sleep nor get scared at the drop of leaves.

While my friends train their muscles to fight and wound, I learn by wisdom to still my peace.

The true strength of a man is judged from his ability to forgive wrong; this is where meekness takes over mighty thrones.

Judge for yourself; who wins? Who loses? And by how much?

I cannot help but think about our world, were peace is fought for from the barrel of guns, and even the man that seeks justice is unjust in his demands.

But can a thing that harms another man be capable of protecting me? If man can cause harm and do not want to be hurt, and can harm without being hurt, then man is the worst of all animals.

22

SERVICE

Services do not proceed from masters but from servants. Masters pay servants for the services rendered according to the satisfaction derived.

For sound and effective services to be rendered, knowledge and dexterity has to be acquired and developed. Although this makes the servant a master of his services, this does not make him a master of his buyers.

Education is the sure hope of the poor. Find the truth and keep it, learn theories and the practice, fantasy as well as reality.

> *Exchanging value for value is all about the business of living.*

Life is very smart, sometimes it wants you to create the value first, and when you can produce it, it pays you back in multiples.

> *Whenever you have something of value to part with, strike a bargain, or else, never complain later that you have been cheated.*

Nobody will pay you the value you do not demand. Watch the timing, an investment that pays you later often pays you better.

"The love of money is the root of all evil, we agree, yet we have millions of it locking in our savings.

Every servant tries to please the master as much as he can and does nothing except in accordance to the will of the master. The first thing we hear from our political office mongers is the determination to serve, but later you realize they actually meant to serve themselves of the public fund. During their campaigns, it is easy to see through the diaphanous layers of their messages, the correct irony of their intentions. In no time they have their hands on the mandate, we wonder if they have exchanged their consciences with Pecunia.

One thing is sure, leadership is service that must proceed from the lowly.

> *If our leaders would discharge their services as servants, then violence will leave the bounds of our nation.*

If only our leaders would abandon the place of masters and cease to see their people as slaves, then they will listen and care for each other as friends.

A simple errand from your people, take what we have contributed and put it to the best use for the good of the people; how mean and shameless our leaders, that they trade their integrity for a few coins. Remember, you did not generate what you squander, the money belongs to the people, and you are failing the very people who trusted you. Violence is a resultant of insensitivity of our leaders to the plight of the people.

Children whose parents are insensitive to their feelings are prone to be violent towards the parents. Students who study in a conducive school environment seldom throw stones at the top of the buildings.

> *Violence is no solution but it is often an easy conclusion.*

War in our nations originates from the leaders especially when they try to play with the mind of their people. Many have started a war in their country just to serve themselves from the opportunities that it will offer not minding the number of people that will loose their lives in the process.

I find no wisdom in being as straight as a pole but much to desire in holding money and friends and treating those two impostors the same. How quickly a man grasps the money that he becomes the enemy of his people.

Productivity is the sure way to prosperity and it is indeed a good thing for a man to prosper if he has given sufficient value for what he has gotten.

The only true spirit of service is love, seeking the good of the people you serve as much as you seek your own good.

23

EXPRESSING LOVE

There are many ways of speaking without sounds and many talks that present confusing signs.

Emotions in man are as diverse as human beings, one from the other in relation to the state of development.

The knowledge we have open avenues to advance emotions and keeps watch over endangering ones,

but no emotion can be sent to jail.

Emotions come right from birth but need reasons to interpret them as they come. Whatever makes babes cry is first interpreted as hunger before any other thing.

When the baby bites the teat of the mothers' breast, does it express fondness or consternation?

Sometimes love may throw stones at the other expecting a smile as a reaction.

Love gives, and gives and wants to give more to take what it gives and to better what it desires.

We love when we give and give when we love to take what we want.

We go where we want and want where we go that our efforts be not in vain, forbid it lord that our acts we cannot justify.

There is no way we would have done that if we were not in love, or did we actually do them because we wanted love? Who says we did not watch it, of course we know when we are in love, we do not need anybody to tell us.

Sometimes love can be bitter and wicked, when we seek it from the wrong people.

There is one thing we often do not realize, that some signals say the direct opposite of what we tend them to say. Not every cut of the eye is a sign of love nor every spank on the back is a sign of hate. Many people find their pleasure and ease saying one thing with the other's term. We may choose to call it an office but it is no sign of strength walking under a false coat.

With reasons we understand the true meaning of gestures, but what happens when the object of our confusion cannot express this in ordinary terms?

When words cannot express what and how we feel, and our gestures are confused?

Many politicians of my dear state take delight in making obscured statements, but what message do you leave when nobody is hearing you?

They call it great wisdom of non-communicable communication.

The best bate of understanding is giving a correct reaction to an action. "When the mother beats the babe in displeasure, does it compliment the message?"

A broken love hurts more than a restored hate can soothe.

When actions are misunderstand, reactions will follow suit. Come to think of it, did you know that your heart is so resilient it won't break if you really do not want it to!

It is safer to stop where you cease to understand.

24

PERFECTION

Be perfect, just as your heavenly father is perfect; is a banner headline in my little book of piety.

Though I have a faith, I do not really like piety as much as I do for adventures.

> *Perfection exists in the work of others because we do not share in the direct vision of the invisible perfect.*

I really do not have a vision if I keep having a different one every other day. What is wrong about yesterday's vision? What if it had come to pass?

> *When a vision is focus, it will unfold hidden features and possibilities.*

Sometimes it is difficult to see well, as there are still many things that you have never seen.

I have never created a perfect thing in my life and I do not think anybody has, not because I do not, but because I know what consists in doing so.

Creativity consists in dragging the invisible reality to the visible world. In doing this, there is a problem;

> *the invisible change forms and expand in detail with every passing time and extended knowledge.*

There is a trap of achievement that many have fallen into, and I must warn you ahead of time. As you remain a student of life, your knowledge is bound to keep expanding and you are going to see new things and old ones differently.

> *Do not jump at every new vision because they look glithering and sparkling nor discard your vision because of unfolding difficulties.*

Vision is like a wide ocean, it is either you stick to your course and get ashore or get lost in wandering and unfolding phenomenon.

> *It is like the love of a goddess, there will always be a new trick to keep you out of your mind.*

Life is a journey, you do not marry every beautiful woman you see in every other town. After all, if she was that beautiful, how come nobody married her? Stick to your wife, the beautiful ones will come from her.

Do not jump at a bunch of gold on the roadside, you must consider why nobody took interest in it all along.

Deceptive schemes do not come as difficulties, they always present themselves as great opportunities and only those as foolish as the fish in the river will not understand that a worm will not float in the water if it is not attached to a string; fools swallow them anyway.

The nature of the picture that you have is consequent of your state of mind and the time you spend to ponder on it. How long you need to do this is not defined.

You can never be perfect unless you define the boundaries of imperfection.

If you can state the imperfect angles of your creation, then you can create a perfect object.

The secret of success is hard work and determination.

You do not need to stare at the image for every detail of your vision less you will get disconnected, but immediately you have enough detail to get you started, tune your mine to stay connected and started working towards the dream immediately. At your designated intervals, stop and assess the relationship of your creation with the image in your mind.

Do not be so mad about slight deviations except when they are spectacular but keep in mind that accumulation of these little deviations may sum to about 180° reducing your effort to nothing. When there are too many inconsistencies in our creation, you are likely to end up creating what you never intended.

Slight changes is your own contribution to the invisible world and a sign that you are on your way to perfection.

> *A broken statue may turn out a great work of art that no artist thought about.*

To be perfect indeed,

> *do not stop until you are delighted by your output.*

If you are not excited by what you have created, start afresh, there is no better way to be good at it than this.

25

CONFIDENTIALITY

Besides your friend, you have a friend who has a friend besides his friend. When you have a friend who cannot keep a secret, then you are likely to fall into a scandal someday.

The bulk of human experience is too heavy to be carried in one mind and is one of the reasons we need friends to pour and share. We need to have confidence in our friends and should be able to say what we mean without fear.

Sharing your troubles and experiences relieve your mind and creates an expansion in your storage capacity of information and the security of these.

> *But a greater burden comes to the mind when we begin to contemplate how many people have got our secret and what they intend to do with them.*

What disturbs human minds the most is what we choose to call 'our personal secrets'. To be relieved of these troubles and have a test of happiness, you need to make some friends and trust in them.

Before you can keep a good friend, there is one thing you must bear in mind;

> *When you confide in your friend, do not expect he will not confide in his friend.*

We have casualties of information leakages everywhere in our society and the one thing that comes to mind is that we only told the information to our friend.

It is true that you only told it to your friend besides the fact that somebody must have had the information without your knowledge, but it is a fact that; the same way the information bugged your mind, it also bugs the mind of the person you told.

When it comes to rumours in life, people are not asked to pay.

Many other people can attend to information management as an office, harbouring bundles of information in moody minds that take the sheen off their faces. The best at these may fall on the bed or while flying on the wings of wine. The best of information reservoir has a single leakage at the bottom of it.

Do not allow these to scare you from friendship but make as many as you can and share the best part of you.

Trust is a burden, I need someone to take my own. If you take too much of it, it can break your neck.

If you cannot choose the confidence you bear, you are going to be dragged into the mud someday soon, as an accomplice of a messy act. But if you give up, that's how you can be given up, why not keep it back.

Do not hide your corn in the poultry farm, look before you leap.

Try the codes on them and know the value of their resistance in other to decide what to share and that worth of reserve.

> *If you had a precious possession or a costly information, you will not trust this to a code of a few combinations.*

Some people are not worth much trust, especially those who have many friends and like to talk. It is better with minds that are trained. Life is not all about evil and secrets but goodness and freedom.

Do not act like a fool,

> *nothing is really hidden in the world.*

Nobody throws his gold in the mud, but we all wallow the mud for gold.

26

EFFICACY

A lot of human minds are very grateful to the body they have, and a lot of bodies do not justify the blessings they have in the mind.

I have seen feeble minds in Atlas and great minds wearing feeble limbs; one part in a complete non-complementation of the strength of the other.

I have seen tiny people moving the world around and the big and mighty slaving in the palace of tiny kings. Big heads like tropical coconut with nothing inside to show.

How do we feel finding efficient men on beggars' seats?

The spirit in the body is more important than the size of the body; the strength of accomplishment is determined by the forces that control the activities of the body.

No man is too poor to be rich, nor any too rich to be poor pending self-management and disposition to the spirit that controls both. Horses do not make holes in the ground, and rabbits do not fly in the air. Nobody teaches a baby to cry, and there are understandings that are not gotten from learning.

Everyday, things happen to us and around us and we either get confused or scream.

A young man refuses to plant during the season, he goes to the temple to complain to God of hunger and poverty during harvest only to come back from the temple and steal for hunger.

It is stupid to beg of God for food as well as ask a hungry man to go and pray. A lazy man is that who will not do the simple things, preparing his mind for that great event that will never come to pass.

If nature had given you the ability to act, do not expect him to act in your place.

It follows that the gods will never do for man those things that man has to do for himself. You can imagine how busy the gods must be at times considering how many people appeal to them for help at the same time, and you can also become a god if you make people depend on you.

But for people who do not have enough patience to wait for fate, the best time is to begin to do what you have to do today. The trees bearing fruits today where planted by men yesterday.

The state of our world is as a result of the efforts of men in co-operation with God. God will not establish peace in our countries unless we start, nor make us the president unless we work to deserve it. God will exalt the lowly to a high position; but God will never install a misfit in a place of authority.

A man who is too careful to make mistakes will never succeed in a thing.

Virtually everything on earth are enemies of man but of them all, man must use to his own good. There are no successes without sacrifices; and if you take too much care of the offerings, then you will fail altogether.

The earth is no food, but for man to have food, he has to sow the seeds and reap the fruits for his upkeep.

The books in your shelf is no knowledge. But for you to have knowledge, you must read the books and force knowledge from it.

Inspiration is a fire, it won't burn without the knowledge acquired through learning.

There is money everywhere and in everything but for you to have money, you must seize one thing and squeeze money from it

The world does not wish you happiness but you must use the world to achieve your happiness. When you pray to God for something, count it not his voice until he tells you he had kept everything for you already and that you should use them for your own good.

Nothing comes into the world and nothing goes out but all circulates around us with some more hidden for you to discover.

If the gods were as lazy as you are, would you bother to pray to them?
They are gods because they do what they have to do and they do them well.

The reason demons deal with men, is because they are too lazy to think and pray.

Dispose all your dexterity and accept the blessing of subduction. The money you need today has already been produced; somebody is keeping it somewhere, go for it.

The men you pass by on the streets have bags of gold and they are looking for whom to pay for what they want.

27

CHOICE

Nature cannot be blamed for human creation nor is nature insufficient in human provisions.

Man sought knowledge from the start and by knowledge, has the ability to decipher the good and bad parts of things in the world. At the middle the world is divided into light and darkness, the choice of which to follow is a man's decision. Nature would have been so insufficient if every man did only good and no less feral if every man championed evil courses.

In our world today, we have the good, the bad, as well as the ugly.

It is human nature to do evil and also natural for man to do good.

Human beings should not be so much blamed for doing evil to their fellow men, but every evil man discovered should be changed, managed or dismissed. If goodness did not have a reward, how many men would want to do it? And how many good men will not enjoy the pleasures of evil only if they would not be discovered. If the gods have no eyes, would you not kill and eat his fowl? After all he won't see you do it.

Many evil men are rendered such by their fellowmen, though the masters of their acts still wear the brows of grace.

Man should not praise himself so much for doing good for it was his nature to do so. A lot of good men are fashioned by their environment of which human character is not independent of, and there cannot be a complete human environment without a fellow man. A good man is judged by his deeds when no one is watching.

The choice of evil is human inclination and the love of good is the work of divine grace.

Man is naturally inclined to evil, the simplest things a man can do while he is living. A lot of men are praised with respect to good works even when it is only fortuitous acts.

Man seldom does those things he knows to be good acts but praises himself when the things he got involved by accident are heralded by others.

Goodness entails sacrifice while evil gives a fake promise of gain. Of good and evil, we have a choice, of what to be and what to avoid. Put your good and evil into the scale and make sure what you want to be balances the weight of what you want to avoid and pulls effect.

But do not confuse nature with the spirit God. The last time I checked, there was not any scale yet produced in heaven to measure the quantity of sin, a single stain upon your soul is sufficient for your damnation, be wise! There are no fools in paradise!

28

JUSTICE

Justice is the best thing that can happen to humanity but the worst thing that can ever happen to a man.

Things go wrong here and there and injustices are poured on humans by their fellow human beings. The scarcest commodity in the world is knowledge, yet it remains the highest commodity claimed by humans. The irony of knowledge is that today you feel you know so much, and just then the light beams a little brighter and you realize you knew next to nothing. The Light is the highest intensity of light, and the only knower of all things.

Rightness is giving good to good and ensuring only evil goes to the evil. But when the judge of the moment lacks the true knowledge, who is right? Consider how many good people we have in our today's world and how many evil ones there are.

There may appear to be many good ones to our senses but they are very few with epignosis of them.

One terrible thing I have seen in the world is that so many institutions have been created to protect the wicked, and few good people in these fighting for the very enemy they are trying to fight against.

Nigrescent minds are hidden under fair skins,

how do you reconcile this? A man can be good within the boundaries that are allowed him by his society. There are some good that will never be done in the world, and the man who finds it to do may be punished with dead.

At a time when the devil himself will appear to many as an angel of light, would you take him for what you see?

It is human to like a good thing when you see one, but better to know them first before you approve of them.

Champions of justice often make victims of the polity, is it a blessing or not?

The band of evil is often seen stronger than the congregation of the saints, it takes the power of God to disband such a mob. A man who does not stand safe against evil should be ready to die to see the good he pursues come to light.

Justice is the first thing a man seeks but the last he wants to be given. Man seeks justice when it appears to bless but gives it out only when he feels by this, he will destroy the other.

One thing about our courts is their ability to discover the truth in the cases before them, but they either pluck leaves to cover this truth or try within their power to avoid it.

The burden of proof is a technical knockout for truth as the man bound for good hardly considers his trail.

A poor man should not go to the court for he has no money to buy what he deserves, but rich men take them there to buy their justice from them.

Because God is wiser than man, He ordains that the crafty is often taken in his device.

When one lawyer faces the truth the other takes to tricks, at the end, lies become the order of the day.

A cockroach was going on his hunt passing along a farm of a thousand birds, I wish you know how long he walked before reaching his farm.

Justice will never be sweet but it is the only thing that can separate evil from good.

29

SILENCE

It is good to talk, but it is better to be silent. You will never be heard unless you talk but a

silent expression is louder than mega sounds.

Concerning the talkative – for that is what we say they are – there is something they ought to know.

It is not in line to talk and think at a time but the best of talks come after enough amount of thought. If you cannot discipline yourself today to think before you talk, you will always find yourself saying things you will live to regret. In the multitude of words is no lacking of sin, using few words to make your point will keep you off the hook.

You must always learn to scrutinize before you publicize.

No time is enough to think but you will hear it is too much of you after some amount of talks. This is to inform you thinking is more important than talking, and

talking is only a partial expression of the findings of thoughts. Learn to minimize what you plan to say, for when the spirit takes control, a thief will condemn himself with his mouth.

You can never condemn a silent mouth but whatever one says is held as evidence against him in the court of law.

What the goat sees but keeps quiet is far more horrible than what the fowl sees and scream.

> *If only you learn to be silent, you will not only save the energy you would spend in talking, but will make a fool of the talker.*

Silence can buy you time, serve you energy and ultimately fetch you power. If you like to play the game of propaganda, let the men do your talking and you can deny consent at your choosing.

Silence is what we learn in response to the circumstances around us. Whatever makes us to talk exercises control over our mouth, and may in so doing drill a leakage in your mind.

> *A leaking mouth will expose the owner to evil, as there are many issues of life that must not be uttered.*

Let whatever you have to say come after a good contemplation on it in either plane or slight offence.

> *Do not give a quick defence to an offensive statement less you implicate yourself in the analysis.*

Talking does not make you innocent nor silence make you guilty. But in all, talk when it is ripe and silent when confused and let this be your personal wisdom.

The spoken word is a spirit being and when it is spoken in faith, it can accomplish seemingly impossible tasks. Words are arrows, do not shoot them carelessly less you shoot yourself without knowing.

When anything seems impossible to you, do not just look at it, speak to it what you want it to be, the visible worlds were framed by the spoken word of God.

30

CONFUSION

It is normal that you should be confused about certain occurrences in life especially when this is the first time you are meeting with such.

You cannot know everything in your life, so there must always be a first time at a task. You have not passed the highway of life before, so approach everything and everyday with caution and expect all manner of strangeness. The truth of life is that strange things will continue to happen in the world, you have not seen them before, they just arrived because their time has come.

Confusion is not an end in itself, but a means to an end. There is one thing you ought to know;

> *people take advantage of you when they discover you are the least confused about the situation you are facing in life.*

Any time you find yourself in a situation you do not like, you become an opportunity for a businessman to make a few coins. Do not be intimidated by those who claim to be wise, know your trade and take your chances. If men had their way, they would make you work for nothing, but as much as you have the opportunity, demand a full price for your service.

But if you can compose yourself and not show off your feeling, then you can be seen as wise even when you have no wisdom in you.

> *The more you are emotional about a problem, the less likely you are going to meet with the solution soon.*

It is an office to be upright even when you are confused but somewhat unwitty not to acknowledge the ignorance that may occur before a confused action.

Learn to drop your anchor in stormy weather, and do not move ahead if you cannot see your way for this is the way of fools. Allow the smoke to clear out so you don't sail by the wind that is not blowing your way.

The wind of confusion has no direction. It never blow one to the solution no matter how near this may appear to be.

Rather, it tends to propel you but to an uncertain destination.

An uncertain place is not the best to visit, but the best to be discovered.

There is a corporate seed to the panacea reaction of a confused situation. You may not easily apply this seed except when it has become habitual or fortunate to have it slip into your memory during the time of action because, confusion tends to trigger a blockage of your sense of reason.

When a man is truly caught in confusion, it is possible for such to forget how to breathe.

In any confusion you may find yourself, just a little moment of silence will bless you with the knowledge of its action.

Some of my friends say you can close your eyes and count from one to ten to relax your mind; but I tell you my friend, you can count from one to a hundred if you want, but keep your eyes wide open for these are dangerous times. Just as it blocks your seat of reason, confusion lets loose your bounds of emotion, you may never be able to establish a blockage unless you know where it is leaking.

Confused people ask a million whys, but questions would not answer the question that already exist in your confuse state. At times the only answer that why receives in a confused mind is a blame on that which does not offend.

Whenever you feel you have done something wrong or more you do not even know what to do, do not avoid control of yourself by taking alcoholics or any other that excites the mind, but you may start with a cup of cold water and then let go the thought and try to reduce your mind to the zero point. When your mind is at zero point, look again between the zero point and where you were, you will discover the wrong turn you made. It may be the least desirable thing you wish to change but you must change it to succeed.

Do not be stubborn to change in life, it is one constant thing you will see and embrace until you quit the planet earth.

31

EXECUTION

A lot of people just do things in life even when they have the least knowledge either of those or the possible result. It is somehow unwise for you to do the things I do or that we should do the things we see others do.

He who wants to do anything either good or evil should first seek to have the knowledge of his action.

The knowledge of your action will give you consolation whatever the result that there may be, since you had the insight that it is what it may possibly be. But do not be too wise to accept your possible error in life, nobody has good knowledge in good time, it is only the work of grace. For many people, business means exertion in the path of uncertainty.

> *He who has no knowledge of his action has no vision of his success.*

Learn to follow the cues of life. People do not close the door behind nothing, nor are barriers placed on the way to nothing. The road may lead to danger, it may even lead to pleasure. Words created existence; everything exists for those who believe.

Be cautious lest you overlook where you should look, once you are inside, the way out may not be that easy.

> *Resist every temptation to go into an act that must be hidden, this is often not the way of wisdom.*

There is a message in every sign, look where you are going. If you ignore the message, be sure to end in a mess. Sometimes it is better not to act at all than to act and fail in what others had succeeded and still succeed.

The person you imitate unquestioningly may be the most ignorant person in his action and you, by virtue of this fact, have double state of ignorance, being ignorant of his ignorance.

In every pre-deliberated act, the result is always visible at the end of the action,

Though reality may wear a variant brow to imagination, it will not be a white elephant of hallucination.

The fact that you did not get what you went for does not mean you should now go for nothing. He who does not plan, it is often said, plans to fail. If you know the secrets of planning, then you can succeed where plans have failed as they often do.

This is one of the secrets, take advantage of every opportunity. The other is to expect the unexpected, and prepare for this whatever it may be.

People seek counsel about the uncertainty in the course they are about to undertake; only to be asked to go ahead for they will understand along the line.

I have seen top executives who take up positions before they learn what the demands of their positions are. The worse is that most of them have no team of advisers; but at times, advice can turn out the worse vice, especially when the recipient has no parameters to determine which to take.

You can laugh at these ones, but how many married couples in your town had training before saying 'I do'? you may even be one of them.

One evil that is present everywhere in the world is that men do not know what they are doing.

Any distinct vision has some object that is incompletely revealed at the start which becomes clear as we advance towards it. There is no natural evil without a sign of danger; poisonous leaves are not bitter for nothing.

But it is very unsound to start when there is absolutely nothing in sight.

Nothing becomes clear except the illucid object of your distant view.

It is not only having the vision of the object, but knowing the better way of going to it.

Going to it alone is not enough, you have to make it your own. You cannot fire a bullet to kill a fly, nor must you raise an army to kill an ant.

You cannot catch the right fish with the wrong net no matter how trustworthy your vision. "It is better never to act, than to act in a way and manner you do not understand. Before you start a war, always look at the strength of your army and weaponry; a swift victory is a sweet victory. When the battle drags for too long, eventual victory may not excite the wearied souls.

Even if every other person does not understand you, you should understand yourself.

Always have a clear vision before you take a step of action, either in the spirit, in your mind, on the pages or before your eyes.

If possible, live as the Chinese do, do not believe what you do not understand. If you cannot see it, you may not get it. A fool is that man who does a thing first and thinks of the consequence later.

There is more wisdom in unsubstantiable omission than a substantiated offense of commission.

32

VISION

Blindness is a disease nobody should desire, but yet it is one abnormality that has come to live with man for ages. To the blind, everything is dark and no direction is worth going but no blind man ever stays in one place forever.

The eye of man is located on the body but his mind sees those things the eye cannot see which are synonymous to the non-existent reality.

You have got a choice between these two undesirable alternatives but different from the horns of the dilemma, since both can be avoided or provided for and at variance one from the other.

One thing you must know is that nobody offers help to the blind, especially one that has his two eyes.

If your eye is not an indispensable asset to the next man, then it is certainly a problem that needs to be solved.

Think of the number of things people try so hard to do in secret, that they would have done in your very presence if only you were blind and then tell me why they should not plug out your eyes from their sockets if only they had their way. If your boss was blind, won't you make him sign over all his money to you seeing he doesn't know what is on the cheque and has no way to confirm?

It is better to be blind on the eye than in the mind.

Vision connects a man to his future, and blesses him with hope in his endeavors.

Corporeal fanatics may have a case to argue here, if there is anything like corporeal fanatism in our society.

The eye of the body sees but limited things while that of the mind has unlimited scope of vision.

The eye of the blind hearted drags him to places and things he does not know but the heart of the blind eyed blesses him with caution of things he does not see.

How careful are you about the things you see? What if you have not seen what you thought you saw, have you thought of this?

I can tell you, if you are always so sure of what you see, someone is going to dupe you big time very soon. The man who is always too sure of what he has seen will soon see what he wants to see to his doom.

The stumble of the blind is no accident but how many accidents do the eyed encounter in a day?

What makes disasters for man is his inability to see the true nature of the things that are visible to his sense.

The caution that the things we see may never be the way they present themselves is very necessary in the conduct of our daily affairs in life.

Partial knowledge excites man to a higher level of emotion since it tends not to present the true angles of danger and caution that may tend to pour some cold water on the burning fire of emotions.

If we allow ourselves to get started at this level, this is when the disasters and destruction is true to come.

Try as much as you can to always envision the invisible part of your vision, that you may be able to maintain a sound level of caution. But a better word of caution is that there is more to this.

It is believed that nobody knows the future, but this is a partial truth. One can rightly envision his future and his end by his present choices and decisions.

It is not every vision that comes through the lenses, more important issues of life are determined by your daily choices.

It is what you sow today, that you will reap tomorrow, it is what you gather together, that you will sell tomorrow.

Life is a vehicle, it does not know where you are going, but is very willing to take you wherever you choose.

33

PATIENCE

Our world has taken to a state of rush that one finds it hard to admit there is still anything good being patient about his affairs in life.

There is hardly an innovation in a machine without consideration of a greater speed of operation.

As the world is moving faster, men are completing their course and appointments sooner.

If a man can still get more things done in his limited time, it will still be a blessing to him, thanks to technology.

It is no bad thing acting at an instance but it is virtuous acting in the best way at the best time.

Amidst the troubles of life,

patience is a blessing to the distressed.

Patience has no yardstick but you can tell how often people say they had exhausted their patience.

Time is very precious I know, but is patience about the time alone?

The only difference between the patient and the lazy and cowardly is what each does while they wait.

While the lazy watches the time tick away, the patient makes improvements on the prevalent while awaiting the ultimate to unfold. If you do not find out and improve the present, you will be so disappointed when the future unfolds.

The opportunities you missed yesterday, if they come back to meet you today unprepared will still be lost like the former despite the number of years you waited for them.

It is true that often the people and things we long awaited only come back and happen a few minutes after we had left.

You may have to ask yourself, do you have to leave before what you wanted appear?

This is not so but only to show how much you adhered to the level of patience that is expected of you and more that no time is too long to wait.

> *The fear and urge for action is the last scene in the drama of patience.*

If you can see the wonder of the fairy tale, it is said, you can take the future, even if you fail.

Fear of losing never makes us gain but those who prepare for the loss that may come often have the better gain of it. Losing the present does not guarantee the future, but improving the present will guarantee a better future. Refusing to take advantage of the present does not convey any advantage for tomorrow, but making careful choices will end any man in glory.

> *He who is not urged to action in a state of distress and confusion is diseased in his emotion but he who controls his emotion is disciplined in the spirit.*

In every storm is an opportunity, to displace the fearful and make room for the confident. In any life storm always grab your lifeline, and do not quit until it is impossible to hold on.

> *The more people fall from the top, the more opportunities for others to rise, but only those who key into the moment.*

Storms never uproot all, it only makes more room for the grounded.

It is good you believe it is going to happen in the very next moment and even if it does not, be happy you waited but never be disappointed you never waited enough.

Jesus Christ said "Watch and Pray", but I am telling you, also wait and look.

There is much to see if only you look again before someone takes advantage of you.

Someone is about to be happy you are not looking, disappoint him and take the day because each time you failed to look, someone steals from you.

This inclination to impatience that does not allow drivers to respect breaks on our highways is very destructive. Motorcycle riders want to arrive before speed machines and it does not help when we want to out-run our legs.

The things that destroy us are those things we find easier to do and those who yield to their inclination loose a favourable summary of action.

There will never be a time the man who goes down will be better than the one who goes up.

There will always be an effort needed for any meaningful achievement in life.

In your search for peace, prepare for trouble. The troubles of life present opportunities for men to earn a living. Since all that men care about in life is how to solve their problems, then the single worthy occupation of the wise should be to present and become solutions.

34

AMBITION

Distractions are necessary oppositions to action and so should not be strong enough to deviate a well directed action, though it varies the receipt intensity.

No medium on earth allows man to put a hundred percent without it taking, no matter how little, for itself.

Consider the cans that preserve and bring your food. They deserve the little they take with them if only you just take what is yours. So is the life of a man who lives to be of service to others. The man who strives with the can to take the last drop, often has his fingers cut and looses blood.

Nothing in fact is ready to serve man so freely but we force the service on them for our own good. And we should not think that those that man have not forced cannot be forced, but only that man has not yet discovered the best way to make it serve him, which you can do if you try.

> *Everything on earth was created to serve man, the gods walking upon the face of the earth.*

Different human beings have different lines of action and so when you champion your own course, do not expect it will not collide with another man's course.

Those who pray to be great must be ready to step on thorns.

> *Those who allow their points to be acted upon without substantial amount of reaction are diseased in their emotions.*

What you now term as hindrances are the opposition the other person's course give to your own course riding over them. You see evil men as wicked, but you understand they wish you were never there to stop them from their course of evil.

Wise people carry extra bags of potentials to overcome this while others get spent and terminated. In all these, if you refuse to be hindered by distractions, you will have the happiness of fulfillment.

Before the gods give their blessings, the man must be ready to prove his conviction; and this he does by sustained effort and determination.

Some more people have decided they will only act in the best place, hopefully where they will never meet any opposition; but James, do not want to be a part of these ones.

The place alone does not make the deal but the time. When you seek the best place, there are demons even in the temple of Jerusalem; where then is the best place?

You make the best place and time and it is no distance from where you are standing and now. Develop a competent resistance to the forces of opposition and get them to obey your instructions. Until you roar at a lion, you will never know how scared it is in your presence.

If you must get to what you want, do not be afraid then to step on people's toes.

Ambition is blind to caution, a one way traffic that does not stop until it is stopped. The ambitious should learn from the wildfire, though it starts small, soon it will be burning down cities.

Those who take a man of ambition for granted pay dearly for it, for the strength of ambition is gathered from little successes. **But any ambition that is not backed by preparation will only lead to frustrations that will end you in rehabilitation.** Remember those who fight and run away will live to fight the second time.

If you are too careful to fight things, do not be too scared of them fighting you.

But in any challenge, be careful of an obvious defeat.

Those who foolishly refuse to accept an obvious defeat will die before their time.

A battle does not make the war, if you are alive, you can fight again and you can win the war. After all, these days, children even try to win the wars their fathers lost.

I also want you to know this ancient wisdom I paraphrased from the art of war, that the victorious strategist only seeks battle after he had secured the victory, either by the strength of his armor or the number of his army, his skills, whatever his faith.

35

LUST

Lust is a natural inclination based on the force of desire that can be trapped at any point of the body below the eye.

> *Sex is relieving yet not without its own burden.*

And it appears there is no relief without its own burden, and no medicine without its side effect, even the ones that are not mentioned.

If it does not have a side effect, then it might not have any effect. For every action there must be a reaction.

Any part of man that does not hunger for its personal satisfaction is diseased.

If you take what you see and desire to take more even what you should not, well then, that's lust. Does it really matter if you call it greed, after all they are twins.

The eye hungers for sight, the ear for sound and the mouth for talk as well as the stomach for food.

It is an office to suppress our desire but it is a dubious claim if anybody has ever succeeded in this fierce battle with himself.

What cannot be cured must be endured and in fact, nature cannot be cured but at best, suppressed and redirected to our own good.

> *All forms of emotion will die of attrition, when you do not give it attention.*

I do not intend to further puritanical affliction, but there is truly in man the power to exercise self-control when spiritual sanity is pursued with a determined will. If you can keep your mind from the thought and your path from its way, then you can keep yourself from the act.

Be this as it may, excuses do not take away the effects of action.

> *If you devote your time and resource to the satisfaction of lust, be sure you spare a little and train your next to carry the burden of guilt.*

Lust is non selective. It catches on any person just as it makes you catch on any person that appears to possess a little potential that ensures your satisfaction.

Lust puts you into thought but does not allow you to get the answer to your thoughts.

Lust makes you pay but does not allow you to demand what you had paid for.

Lust makes you have hope even when all hopes are obviously dashed.

> *Lust makes you act even when in action there is danger everywhere.*

Who is that man that wants to punish the sins of passion when all caution went on vacation? Why are you asking him for reasons, or did he not tell you that it was a rainy day and reason was not at home? Any man can misbehave when he cannot be caught.

Lust is a conniving sneaky bastard that creeps to consume its cravings whenever reason looks the other way.

Precarious acts often do not present a positive result. In a time that can be compared to a lightening flash, Lust evaporates leaving you with the reality undesired. What is left is sense of guilt that hangs over you like bags of bricks.

The best thing to do at this time is to own-up to your mistake. If you try to cover the deed of your hand, you would only be committing other acts guilt-worthy and foul and that is how it accumulates.

When a man's eye is fixed on higher goals, he will gradually be lifted above the lure of base things. The mind cannot be empty, so to keep it pure you must fill it with proper thoughts.

An idle mind is the devil's workshop, for the spirit of men neither slumbers nor sleeps.

There will never be a successful revolution without a tangible mental liberation and successful re-orientation.

36

HOLINESS

Cleanliness they say is next to holiness and holiness is next to godliness.

A clean container will always have the least relative weight.

A clean container has nothing to hide nor is it ashamed of itself.

Cleanliness in thought is good for the human mind from where proceeds good and evil.

By our faith, good is spelt and defined, differentiating it from what we term evil.

The good acts are supposed to make us clean and by virtue of being clean assume holiness.

Even though I have some doubts about this,

I know that doing good makes a man feel good, only after the good has been done.

Nobody can benefit from a venture he has not started however lucrative the prospect. Until you make efforts to be holy before God, you can never enjoy the pleasures of a holy life.

Holiness, apart from the claim that it makes man a potential candidate for heaven, is good for the human mind.

Holiness is one good habit that is worth cultivating, it produces a healthy mind and body.

A life without sanctity will end in bitter agony.

Man needs peace and the first must be within himself before the society comes to play.

To whom much is given, it is said, much is also expected.

By virtue of the knowledge that exists in you, you had established a standard for your personal judgment of your acts.

By virtue of the knowledge of good that exists in your mind, every evil act is a war against your own standard which is transform into a standard measure of guilt that you either face or is stored away in your mind.

Quilt stored away canvasses for some more quilts within which they form a coalition opposition to your smooth mental deliberations and executions with resultant *crises de conscience*. No sooner the opposition gains enough force, it takes over the control of you and the evil part of you rules over the good.

See for yourself who you would look like if your emotions take your reason captive. How would you feel if the soul, the captain of the mighty being abandons control, then the ship will begin to wreak havoc and end in calamity; when you should find yourself complete the action before you understand what you are doing.

But James, take up in your hands the control of yourself and let nothing happen except that which you had decided.

> *When a man is drowned in the pool of bad conscience, he can easily become a ready tool for evil.*

> *If you hold yourself in a holy compunction, you will have within you the lightest conscience.*

Conscience! That most resilient voice from within, often ignored and hard suppressed, yet, never giving up.

A bad conscience is a deadly affliction, and many who cannot swallow the bitter pill of truth die from it.

37

CHARITY

Charity begins at home but must not end there. The spirit of charity is not purchased but developed from little things. Nobody has too much to want nor does anybody have too little to give.

> *The best thing to do when in want is to give out even the very little that you have.*

I used to be happy when men give to me until I discovered the harm I was doing to myself. The joy of a receiver is short lived, but that of the giver last forever. When I discovered this secret, I began to give and my joy knows no bounds.

> *No matter what you lack, never lack what to give! What you receive will fade away, but what you give will live forever. A gift that has been given never loses value to the giver, but that which is received will fade away no matter the value we place on it.*

The most important aspect of charity is the State of mind of the giver and not what we actually give or its amount.

Charity is the expression of love and not a display of wealth. I give this warning to friends, those who will care to take; that if you do not give out of love, it will benefit you more if you do not give at all.

You do not need to have enough before you start giving and indeed, nobody ever admits having enough except in boasts.

Your sight of a fellow human in need of help is supposed to arouse some desire within you to help the person overcome the problem. He who does not feel this is diseased in the spirit.

Tiny organisms never leave any of their specie in a state of problem, outstanding is the ants. Compare how many ants can measure your weight and size and judge for yourself the amount of love for your fellow is expected of you compared to what they have.

He that shows no charity, has no inner passion.

Remember the golden rule; "do to no one what you would not like done to you" and to any man what you would expect another person do to you if you were in his state to be precise.

Do not force charity out of any man and resist any attempt by any man to force an act of charity out of you, but do not forget that, it is naturally expected of you.

The world depends on you, right from the man living the next door.

If you can do it, you are the only one that can do it, if you can feel it, you were the one destined to do it.

Do not try to shift your responsibility and try as much as you can not to disappoint your nature that nature may not disappoint you.

He that is thus charitable, has a sense of human sympathy.

38

PERFECT CHARITY II

In every human undertaking, there is a boundary between perfection and imperfection which has never been crossed and may never be crossed but expected.

Charity is a vocation, an expectation and an undertaking that has what constitutes its state of perfection.

Some people find themselves doing acts which are later termed charitable while others find themselves in the midst of charitable people and simply dance to the music to avoid oddity.

Some more people find themselves in love with acts of charity at one time in their lifetime and seek to actualize it to their very best. Here, uncertainty of what constitutes the best part of the act makes their emotions to dwindle.

> *He that wants to be perfect in charity should learn to do everything to his own loss but rather to God's glory.*

At the best of human effort, his acts of kindness are selfishly motivated.

The best way to start up charity is to nurse a selfish motive, and when you are thus saturated by your cookies, begin to follow your heart. Maybe givers never lack, or maybe he that sprays his bread on top the waters will have it back after many days, probably multiplied.

You can be known as a good man if people feel your charity, and someone you help today may be the only one to help you tomorrow, just something selfish and nice and your office of charity has just open for business. And better still you can enjoy the love of many friends, the portion of a man who gives gifts, only you must be careful you do not run short of supplies.

When you use gifts to win friends, they will certainly abandon you in your difficult times when your giving would cease.

We all have a faith either in the abstract or concrete things.

The source of faith is the God for us who deserve the best from us just as we deserve the best by virtue of our faith.

What law finds application in discrete particle finds its application in the bundles

though with variations based on changes in condition and state. If the law of conservation of energy ever applies, then there is no gain or loss in the world.

We gain from our loss and loose from our gain at different times that constitutes the portions of our life stretch. When your gain today is a loss, then prepare for your loss tomorrow which will be a gain to balance up nature.

Someone or something gains each time you lose, and somebody somewhere is suffering the loss that constitutes your gain. If you can picture how empty the end of life is, then you can imagine the evil in accumulating wealth to the detriment of men.

For every charitable act, there must always be a man at the receiving end.

Whatever is done to a man is done unto God, be it evil or good.

Let him who wants to be perfect in acts of charity also learn to dismiss from his memory his acts of kindness to humanity.

Do not count your loss or measure your gain.

Where our strength limits us is where the strength of God starts to fill us.

If you cannot give what you want to give, then do not give it at all. But if you must give, then understand this; that it is going away and you will never have it again.

Spread your bread on the waters and you would ever live picking bread in your lifetime.

You do not need to start with the whole world, just the man the next door and the whole world will take care of their needy ones.

If the whole world had equal share of nature, it would then have been the worst place to stay in.

Interdependence is the best spice of human community.

If you know how quickly men fall from glory, then you will be careful with the needy. Life is full of surprises, you can never be too sure of tomorrow.

39

GOODNESS

It is good to be good even when goodness attracts the opposition of the evil.

> *As you cannot take lemon without enjoying the goodness of lemonade, so also, you cannot do good without feeling good as a reward.*

Goodness defines evil based on human feeling devoid of essence.

The real essence in goodness is human simplicity.

You know that you came into this world with nothing, and will certainly leave this world someday taking nothing along with you.

Even if God was not watching the acts of men, I know this very well, that it is good to be good.

> *You will never know how good it is to be good till the day you stand in need, but the problem with many people is that they are too quick to forget.*

A man strives to be good that he may attract goodness in return not because he really likes the idea of being good at all.

> *Even the mouths of evil sing the praises of good and punish evil in double return.*

A thief is often the first to slap a thief, maybe because the other was too careless to be caught.

You are a good man if you cover another man's nakedness, but may end up as an accomplice if you cover his carelessness.

Goodwill is established by conviction in faith in a thing that has no substantiation.

A man will have all that he has given out if you make a mistake of telling him you will double the return, but same may never give one in a thousand if convinced he will never get it again in life or death.

Give all you may afford to the next man and do not expect even a good word of appreciation from him.

If a man throws what you have given him to the mud and asks from you another, would you give to him?

If you had all the powers to make him pay for what he has done, would you desist from it? And come to thinks of it, the last talent that God gave to you, where is it? Yet here you are always asking from God; and when you do not get it quickly, you begin to complain.

Do not be afraid of death if by goodness you block the evil from getting to the public pot for they like taking the lion share. Goodness pays back in cool coins but evil pays his own with hot notes that set their recipients in mad gears that we observe and feel envious.

A stray sheep will always come back with pot belly but for how long will she escape the lion's claws.

When you see a thief run in flashy cars, ask him how many bullets he escaped the last night.

Evil tends to give your life wants but take from you the most needed.

When a man of goodwill is troubled and afflicted, let him remember that the good deeds where not to his own loss and that the evil thought, if actualized, will never be to his own gain.

When evil tells you what you will gain, try and ask him what he will take in return.

The least he would want to take would be the means of enjoying what he gives to you.

I have seen men struggle so hard in the name of living behind a legacy for their children, and when I looked closer at their wisdom in these acquisitions, I discovered they have missed the fundamental.

There is a better legacy in those things you leave in your children, and not the things you leave for your children.

If you teach your children how to fish, you would not struggle so hard to live behind a pool of rotten fishes.

You have a choice!

40

KNOWLEDGE

Knowledge is the soul of character and experience the soul of policy.

Let the fool never make claim of wisdom or he will never taste of wisdom in his lifetime.

Always hang your bag where you can easily grab it on your own for having to use a stool is a disgrace to your stature and sense of wit.

> *Know what you know, and to acquire wisdom, seek for the knowledge of the rest as you cannot be wise with partial knowledge.*

You can safely deny ever being a military man if you cannot stand the blow of a soldier boy.

> *The knowledge you have makes you a prisoner of the things you do.*

It was better for you when you did not know, but now you know, so, your sins remain with you.

But don't be too quick to conclude, ignorance is your costliest liability on earth, and that you choose not to know means that you know what you should know, and that is your sin. Ignorance is safe and stupid for whoever has attained the age of wisdom.

Real safety does not consist in avoidance but pretense; for

> *real enemies will attack even a fallen man.*

To do what you know is wrong is to be dishonorable before yourself.

To be dishonored by yourself is to be disconnected from defense and pray that while you plead, you are not faced by attack.

The things you say make you a prisoner of the way you live.

When a man has made a foolish claim, he finds himself struggling to live up to it for fear of shame.

It is good to be a preacher but many preachers dishonor the office of preaching.

First it was public speaking and now, public preaching, the ability to stand before the public and lie convincingly without a single feeling of remorse.

Do not let the devil preach to you lest you repent.

To say what is good is virtue consisted in facing the truth that proceeds from your superego. When you have the knowledge of truth, then be wise enough to seek revelation, there is much to life the eye cannot see.

Many are scared to talk of goodness not because they do not know their essence but because they had been taken by evil simplicity.

Political office leavers talk of moral constraints instead of moral acts, for that will encircle them with rounds of jeer.

Any man who can do evil, is also capable of good, it is only a function of willful determination.

Do not build around you a fire you cannot extinguish. If you will not live to your word, it is better you are quiescent; but more dishonorable to be quiet when you should be talking.

> *There is much pressure in the world to make you think of the search for knowledge as a waste of time considering what you want, but it is the other way round; it is the more knowledge you have, the more time you save.*

Wisdom sharpens the axe, while ignorance is a waste of time, energy and resources.

Do not just know one thing and go to sleep; if you have your way, try to know everything, it will help you a lot in life.

41

OCCUPATION

It is all vain things that charm the life of man. Happy at birth and sad at death, coming with nothing and with nothing transits.

The soul we say is neither born nor death; little wonder if it increases or decreases by our labor for knowledge. If you understand the essence of the spirit and the soul upon the earth, then you will better understand the true business of life.

Living the fate of immortality in the hands of mortal beings full of frailty, has become a cause for serious concern.

From age to age the search continues, man seeking to own the knowledge of himself and with the little he has, what does he do with them?

A little advice to the man who seeks to know, that you cannot discover yourself from the volumes of books written by the arts and sciences, but by looking within and asking from God.

We may find ourselves at one time contemplating what the benefit there is in the knowledge mentality of humanity if in all of it the world cannot have the peace of intelligence.

The way of peace is truth, the revealed truth that handles hidden facts.

We may choose to call this mental busyness that seems to establish the difference between the state of illiteracy and literacy, and what a crisis when a man does not even know what he knows.

When a man is doing more than a thing at a time, it is a sign he does not know what he should be doing, and he may not excel in any.

By knowledge man wages war against himself as well as stop the war in sight.

Intelligence does not give a peace assurance as the ignorant survive alongside the informed.

If you can earn enough to solve your problems, and much left to acquire your pleasures, what a blessing you have.

But my friend says there will come days of trouble, shouldn't we prepare for this?

However, there is nothing as good as peace of mind.

We labor and spend pulling weeds but yet the weed will grow again.

We wear and tear thinking the meaning and find its vanity pulling weeds at all.

Vanity indeed for a narrow mind but this I wish you would never be.

The very day you plant a farm, you begin the struggle with weeds; the very moment you come alive, you begin the struggle to survive.

There is a more bitter struggle to stay on top than you struggle to get to the top, have this also in mind.

Be pleased indeed with the difference and not the feeling of success in your undertaking.

My friend, before I forget, if you can solve your problems and earn your pleasures, be happy with this. But security, there is no security, you are not protected, not even from yourself.

Compare the past to the present and if there exist a difference, make it a happy recall of a lifetime.

A single viable seed makes a difference in a bag of a million death ones.

A little brilliant light makes a difference in the darkest night.

What changes the tone of history is no thunder storms but a little brilliant light.

Do not be too scared to do what has never been done, there is no better way to distinguish yourself in life than this.

Do not try to change the whole world for you will present a greater task, but just a single man and allow the sequence to take a natural course. This is how the world will change its own self.

In these entire life vain struggles, it is your contribution that will make the difference.

Man does not so much fancy the success, but that little difference between the past and the present.

42

SELF

Do you know who you are?

You find your peers retort in minor upsets, "who are you?" And the other possibly returning with similar gestures.

> *It is a different matter when you know a fellow man, but life begins to make sense when you know yourself.*

My greatest fear in life is that right inside of me is an unlimited potential.

> *I am not afraid of what I cannot be in life, but what I can become if I am committed to it.*

We live in a world of endless possibilities, nothing can really stop a man who is determined to forge ahead.

A good number of human beings do not know who they are and if you do know, be happy because you have made a difference.

You have known nothing so far in life, if by now you have not known the truth of who you are, not what you have made yourself or others have made you.

Until you have the knowledge of yourself, you will be living on the opinion of others; and this is where you begin to fail in life.

> *Who you are, is not titular nor official but autojustific and spontaneously expressive.*

A lawyer strives to assume the position of a justice when in reality he is a good law magician. A jack of all trade is a mediocre born to be, the man who knows too much will never make much progress in life.

There is no need confusing yourself, a good sex hawker assuming the celibacy of the nunnery. I heard you say she is born again, or was it born against? They are one and the same any way, but I tell you she would do better if only she is afraid of the man standing next to her.

One of the problems of personality is that we tend to mix passion with action and love with lust, we confuse our feelings and misunderstand our actions.

You are safe in passion as much as you can be in action but never take-up the two at the same time.

If you are a victim of passion, why bother about action? And if you must take to action, why take passion into consideration. If you are a man advancing at a girl, why not stop and think what you feel and want from her. If all you have in stock is lust for what she can give, why bother to confuse yourself talking of love.

You cannot bend a tree without bending yourself; you cannot confuse a sincere mind without confusing yourself.

It is a bitter truth that whatever thing you do to others, you do better or worse to yourself. **There is no better way to prepare for success in your enterprise than as you handle the enterprises of others.**

Many men who earned evil at the end of their affairs had evil intensions from the start. It would be quite safer paying the much you can afford for the object of your lust and allowing it to end as soon as it no longer meets your desire.

Love is food for thought and the star that mars if not polished to taste.

Love establishes a river in the heart that may run through the eye for years before it finally dries if suddenly cleaved.

Spare yourself the trouble of feeling guilty and spare the heart of others some phobic mars. You cannot just continue to be confusing what you say with what you mean.

People who do not know what they want in life always spend
a good deal of their time, energy and resources paying for
things they never needed.

It starts from knowing who you are, this is the only way you can know exactly what you want.

Much of the things people pay for is a pitiable waste, they do not need them and will never need them in their lifetime.

If only you can try to separate them, then you have a true knowledge of your person.

Your word is a seed; if you throw it to the ground, it will grow. And anything that grows has abundance of hope and never wishes to die young.

You sowed that seed the day you threw it into a fertile ground. You do not buy personality; you earn it by your actions.

You are only who you are till the day you can afford to be the other.

Do not confuse yourself with what you are not even when you can be whatever you want to be.

43

GREATNESS

It is good to learn from the experiences of your predecessors.

The youths of today are too wise in their thinking to learn even from their mistakes.

It is actually sad what you would expect from the president of a country that does not have a constitution, for so it is with men in charge of a large entity like self, yet without a principal guide.

How sad if you should observe how you hire and fire yourself at will without recourse to the effects they all have on you. How many bad choices people make even with the warning staring glaringly at them.

The greatest form of abuse perpetrated on earth is the abuse of self.

Though mistaken acts lead to great discoveries, some mistakes may be too costly to be paid for.

My father told me of people who bend trees to set traps and even pestles to make bows and these stories are neither true nor false.

Great men existed before greatness was established and even exist to set new thresholds for what can be considered as greatness.

The secret of the saints consists in the nothingness of life, but we must understand that advocates of evil believe in this too, but with emphasis on the lives of others.

And of a truth, life is nothing when you take out the purpose.

It can be likened to the game of soccer when you take out the goal post. However entertaining you may want it to be, you will soon come to the stark reality that it made no sense if you scored no goals.

> *Life is only meaningful when you live it in pursuit of something of value.*

Our people say that condition makes crayfish to bend and too much on the part of fire make the corn to explode.

> *The Saints were never perfect beyond distractions and accidentals, but they refused to be hindered by them. A mind that is focus on purpose will spurn the distractions of the storms of life.*

I see the saints not as people who lived their lives totally without falling victim of what the world knows as sin, but more as ordinary people who handled the ordinary aspects of human life in an extraordinary way. Any form of greatness that does not affect the welfare of other men in a positive way is only a scarceness of understanding.

> *Distractions should not lead to distortion except for minds without strong focus.*

But how can a man have a focus when he is looking at nothing, when he cannot see something worthy of getting. With a good foundation any man can build a tower, you only keep building blocks on top the other and before you know you are visible from everywhere.

Do not let faith deceive you, nobody hopes for nothing; there would be no Christian on earth if heaven was not a mansion big and beautiful. And the best part of the deal is that once you get in, you will never be thrown out.

> *Accidents are resultants of poor concentration, not signals of wrong adventure.*

> *And no concentration can scorn distraction without a strong conviction.*

Whenever accidentals occur, there is a need to redefine your vision and shift back from possible deviation.

> *The only end point of any mission is the object of primary inspiration.*

And unless you get to this, do not think of any termination though the urge may come from within due to factors without, but a stop at any other point is a sign of weakness. If you faint in the day of adversity, then your strength is small and you were not prepare to win.

> *Dirt is only found on the surface and given as good reward to lazy diggers; but he that digs deep enough is often given the pleasures of precious stones and metals as well as spring of clean water for thirst.*

Whatever cannot stop the sun from rising should not stop you. You do not fire your cause in the face of a storm, because you may never know how close you are to the shore; I even heard that close to the mark is where the demons pitch their tents and the darkest hour comes before the glorious dawn.

Your attainment of your destination can only be delayed, you cannot be stopped unless you stop.

Death is not the end of a well-defined vision; it even spreads faster and wider after the death of a good visionary.

> *Three things will determine whether you will attain to any height of greatness in this life, the love in your heart, the service in your hand and the motive in your mind.*

You cannot get higher working the lower; you can never earn a token of importance solving unimportant problems.

44

LABOR

There is dignity in every human labor.

The bishop is no less important than the mass servers nor is the governor more important than the street cleaner.

It is because man is not content with his position that he starts to develop envy of the positions of others.

One of the greatest human problems is the awareness of self and the proper estimation of true worth.

It is because we envy the position of others that they become higher than ours.

It is because we accepted they are higher than we are that we struggle and kill ourselves to be there.

Why will they not steal all the money from the treasury when we make too much noise that they realize our weak points.

The gain you derive from your labor is the dignity of it.

You may argue that not all labors bring gain to the workman, but if the society can benefit from your strength, you have the greater part of it.

You may argue your gain is not as much as that of the other, but you are yourself and the other is himself.

If you could work a little smarter, sell your services to who has the kind of money you want to pay for it, you can get more for less.

Solve problems and solve important problems. Improve on the solution offered by others and keep improving for greater pay. Be happy within you if you can realize the game is worth the candle.

If you seek the knowledge of the dignity of your labor, then do this to yourself; compare the joy of motherhood to the pains of pregnancy and labor.

Every good thing has its pains and joys.

> *If you seek a paying line of business, then tag along the line of men's pleasures or ask your pay when men are in pains, and watch as strong men let go of their spoil.*

When a man's pain is intense, he is bound to let go of whatever the grip, the same with pleasure. The more a man needs a thing, the more easily he will part with his cash.

Two options there are in all human affairs option A is a sweet coated codeine while

> *Option B is a bitter coated sweet.*

Unwitty men choose option A because it first comes to the mind, this is to say, they fall in love with the sweet part of life at their tender ages and live with the bitter core for the rest of their life.

Wisemen summit themselves to the bitter rigorous part of their choice through formation with intense heat and pressure, and live with the sweet core for the rest of their lives.

> *If you are not humble enough to be an apprentice, then you are in no way worthy to be a master.*

There is no option C.

Just like pregnancy, it starts sometimes, and ends sometime. Unless you take it to the end, you loose the joy, and consequently bear the burden of guilt.

One more thing James, If you take the sweet part first, how bitter the bitter part will be and at the closing part of your life, but if you allow the bitter part to come first, the remaining sweet core will present to you the sweetest experience anybody has ever had. Try this with sugar and bitter leaf. You have a choice!

45

SOCIETY

There is one slang I do not so much fancy; it is the "I don't care" that we often use. A man can define the society and the society can define man. If you do not work to change your surroundings, then your surroundings will change you by whatever means.

> *The head does not ache for nothing, there must be some part of the body that is out of order, and the head is only drawing your attention.*

If you cannot ignore the headache when it comes, then do not ignore the signs around you, they are not there for nothing. When nature in its wisdom puts signs on things, be they beings or beasts, it is so that you may observe them to your own safety. But if you ignore them, it is at your own peril.

> *Learn to obey the signs, even the most stupid of them, no matter how much of a hurry you are in; a stupid sign can save your life!*

Every other man is important and you would not have had the best experience if you were the only man on this island. Sometimes the teeth might bite the tongue and quarrel over issues now and again, yet they still stay and work together in the mouth, the kind of unity we need in our world.

You have the right to get anything for yourself in life but must not, as a necessity, deprive the other person of the little he has. The feelings of others at most times are important but must not dictate your own feelings.

> *If what gives you peace does not bring joy to others, check the course of your action.*

While you stroll to the mouth of the stream to fetch a little water for yourself, turn at the waves rising behind you and observe what they say.

Clean and healthy water will not talk in turbid waves, but if turbid waves result, go some other way or never fetch.

One difficult thing for man is for him to give a check of himself in life. It is difficult to face the truth in life when you are looking at an obvious gain. So many men forget about integrity the very moment they are trusted with public funds, check them well!

Man feels the best way for him is to just push on and on without re-examining if he is on the right track.

> *A man who is not going the right way is obviously going nowhere, this often does not occur to the man except later with some bitter regrets.*

There is a reason the people are not happy about your feeling of peace and fulfillment;

> *You possibly have not done it well or have done what you should not have done.*

There are rules of living which are more or less natural laws of action and consequences.

One of these laws is taking undue advantage of the less privileged, and making a blunder of a public trust. You cannot justify yourself in this kind of act no matter how good you are in the art of persuasion.

Though many people still believe in sadomasochism, it is not the best part of a man's life. You have to care about the feelings of others towards you in your local community.

There are no universal definition of what constitutes good and evil in the world, but only consequence of the reaction of the people to such deeds based on how it affects them.

Rules are made for order, while manners are reactions to disgust.
Morality they say is a function of the stomach and the skin. If it doesn't ache the stomach or hurt the skin, maybe it's the right thing to do. But without a standard guide in life, every rule is bound to end in error.
You may choose not to give a damn but be sure to damn the flow.

You will never know the importance of attitude until you see a champion deserted;

some cannot bear the turn of events, and die sooner from depression.

46

DISCIPLINE

It is funny that man goes to a fight that he cannot win, yes, for this is what it is, fighting with the very determinant of your strength.

Had it been others, I would approve of the threat, but you, my acquaintance, my friend, myself. What is it you can hide from me and from where do you hope to launch your secret attack that I will not know.

The hardest war on earth is war with yourself

Though fierce the war may seem, it is not enough reason to allow an uncontrolled flow of you. The worst happens when you cannot even discover that you are wreaking havoc on yourself. A man who cannot see food and walk away is likely not to go far in life, and may likely die before his time.

Excesses are signs of indiscipline and discipline consists in the effective control of your members.

Many great minds had rather avoided it than go fighting.

You may argue what made their minds great, but it is because they were able to take a decision that best suited their understanding of human situation and existence.

The harassment, they had been constantly confronted by themselves, is what we should not desire, for whoever fights and run away shall live to fight again.

Avoidance of you is a choice but confronting yourself is the solution. If you do not confront yourself, it will confront you at your weakest point.

The weakness you do not challenge will challenge you; and the bad you do not disgrace will disgrace you. The erroneous aspects of your life have to be changed while the corporate parts need to be encouraged.

This is not a war that you will permanently win, but with good management of your personal conflicts, you can have the joy and fulfillment of discipline.

You may not yet attain the status of a general if you cannot recruit yourself fully to the course of your destiny, and stay on till you win the war.

He who feels he has conquered himself might possibly be ignorant of his guilt. You may argue there is no guilt in ignorance but be assured there exists the ignorance of personal guilt in the day to day conduct of people's life affairs.

I saw one fat potbellied man laugh at a drunkard who was staggering his way home, and I imagined who has committed a greater sin or will pay the bigger price, is it the drunkard or the glutton?

Get the rebellious parts of your life in chains and only allow them to proceed after you had deliberated and found them necessary for the particular situation.

The first stupid man I saw on earth was eighteen years. He was just old enough to make mistakes; for of all the knowledge he acquired, nobody thought him about himself, the very empire he was assuming control, and he never bothered to learn.

47

SELF II

I understand how you feel about the madness that has just come to town. The personality crisis that has had a firm grip of simple men, making them see kafter cheap popularity for incipient reasons.

The monkey may resemble the gorilla in many aspects but a monkey is a monkey and the gorilla, a gorilla.

> *The fact that a cat has ventured into the forest does not mean it will come back as a tiger,*

nor will Noah's flood clean the spots on a leopard's skin.

Even with abundance of rain, the zebra still retains its stripes. Our inability to realize who we are and the non-appreciation of our person, for those who have cared to realize, have made us to seek confusion we would well have avoided.

> *You have been created in the image of God, and you are like God.*

Unfortunate, there are very few books that are available to tell you about specifically you. But there is a testimony that you can believe, the testimony of God about Himself and you.

If you realize you are like God, he is your father, then like Father like son. If you have the power of God and the faith of God, then nothing shall be impossible unto you.

You are wondering who you are, this is a little simpler than you have made it; find out who your father is.

You cannot know about yourself if you do not know about God your Father.

> *When you know which tree produced the seed, then you can tell what it will grow into all things being equal.*

The truth about you is in God, the more you know about God, the more you will know about yourself.

It might be true you would have been this had it not been that, but take it that for now you are not, and will not be until you are.

> *The most stupid thing that has happened to humanity is that goats prefer to be titled and addressed tigers and tigresses especially in our contemporarily society.*

With increased population and limited accommodation the world is gradually Turning into a jungle, and survival is the order.

Titles are part of human adaptation, a survival technique, don't mess with your chances.

I have seen laboratory attendants claim the position of medical doctors and assistant lecturers with B.Sc. claiming the qualification of professors. These claims lead them to doing things beyond their strength and a lot of them destroy themselves in the process while many others are confronted by their inefficiency.

It is not a wrong spirit that aims at higher things but such must also be content with the things at hand and use them to get to what you want.

> *Sudden jumps result in broken limbs,*

while slow and steady wins the race.

Patience with an appreciation of himself made the toad to capture the lion of the ibibio mythology.

Before you assume what you are not, ask yourself, "does your claim of a tiger give you the claws of a tiger? In everything, be yourself.

You cannot be who you do not know, that is your confusion.

But to be who you were meant to be, find out first and put it as a big picture in front of you; look at that picture every day and in due time, with sincere effort, you will win the war of self-transformation.

Do not wear a shoe that does not size you lest you fall to your shame. Do not confuse yourself.

48

KNOWLEDGE II

Intelligence is a gift of nature but it is not a guarantee to a height of greatness. Every man must utilize his intelligence in order to achieve whatever he wants to achieve in life.

By intelligence, we learn to code and decode different signals that come to us from both the living and our non-living environment.

We learnt the hard way never to put our hands into the hole to catch a crab no matter how much you needed it for dinner because many things are possible; you can be seriously bitten by the crab, the hole may be occupied by a dangerous snake and many more dangers you could expose yourself. Instead we learnt to seek out the content, making them do just what we want them to do. It is wisdom to make those things you can't go to come to you of their own accord.

Knowledge is good for man even when it is the reason of his fall. It also makes man to rise if properly received and managed in the right direction.

Knowledge is received by acts of communication. It does not just flow into the head but has its origin from the visible and invisible existence who themselves cannot claim to be the original owners of knowledge.

> *According to Confucius, to go too far is as bad as to fall short. And conquests and acquisitions are useless if a man cannot benefit from the products of his success.*

Pitiably enough, at the end of all this life struggle, the only thing you take with you is only that which you had given away, the only knowledge that dies is the one we hold to ourselves and take them to our graves, these ones are lost forever.

Communication is a direction of signals that can only have effect on close circuited decoders fine tuned to the frequency of the transmitter. This is why not all the students in a lecture hall receive the knowledge in a lecturer's explication.

> *The secret of knowledge and wisdom consists in daily preparation.*

Repetition they say, strengthens the memory. The knowledge you have well-received may get buried beyond your reach even inside you if not properly managed at the surface by daily visitation and practice.

Knowledge does not come to man with all the glories of its Kingdom but its glories are revealed to any man that shows sincere devotion to its teachings of hard work and dedication. The true glory is only revealed to the man who sincerely runs with the vision.

> *It is the secrets of knowledge that constitutes the foundation of success.*

Success, yes, success is the greatest motivation available to any man.

> *A man that succeeds in tiny deeds will never fail to attempt bigger ones.*

Anything that succeeds will grow be it good or not. That fruit, success, makes men daring and mad.

Every good master was once a servant learning to rule by his obedience to his master.

A man that has earned his kingdom has likely earned with it also the proper way of directing his subjects. The fall of many kingdoms has always come from kings who were never trained for the office. A man who is never trained to keep what he will eventually inherit will as soon as he gets such inheritance begin to lose it.

It is only in righteousness that any kingdom can endure forever. Any knowledge that is not truth will eventually perish, scientific facts become helpless in the light of better illumination.

> *Attend to knowledge for a year and it attends to you for a century. No natural knowledge is complete, the more you stir, the better you become.*

It is wisdom to acquire knowledge but knowledge is an ambivalent master. It is from the same that comes good and evil.

49

LABOR II

Every human enterprise is profiting to the entrepreneur. Whatever the profit may be is a reciprocal of the recipient of your labor.

Even loss is a profit to an entrepreneur because it gives him a gain of caution in future endeavors.

Many young men roam shrines and temples seeking solution to their non-productive labor according to their understanding. Negative by positive is negative and positive by negative is negative thus my teacher made me to understand.

Negative by negative is positive yielding profit though surprising, but the wrong thing done at the wrong time is benefiting to the individual for it gives a true test of ignorance.

> *If your labour does not yield you profit, it is either you have done the wrong thing at the right time or the right thing at the wrong time.*

We agree there is time for everything but this is only for the simple mind. I tell you in the words of the master;

Now is the favorable time, today is the day of salvation.

Time is precious, gain it, don't waste it, just watch how much you give. Work with the time you have, it is one currency on earth that you can never accumulate.

A little portion of the time you spend sleeping is what others have used to attain greatness; so you can sleep even more, only be sure to wake up and meet poverty.

Great minds manipulate the times and the seasons to suit their wills and purpose.

Men have planted vineyards in the desert, industries have defied the sleep of night, **there is no natural boundary that cannot be overcome.** We may grand this stealing from nature, but who is it that has never stolen from nature if taking what is not yours is stealing in reality?

Let a man waste your money, but not your time; money can be refunded, but time once lost, is gone forever.

One more poison eating the minds of the people, is ignorance of the very reward of their labor.

Rewards are no subject to persuasion especially when it has to come from invincible nature.

Evil actors should learn to absorb evil reactors for deeds and consequence follows the rules of nature.

I only pity any good that is not proactive, for experience has shown that reaction is often too weak to be felt when once you have been beaten on the head.

Do not expect it to come softly from evil, for to any evil man, it is dangerous to fail, learn from the thief next door.

He who toils at night should prepare to smile while he who sleeps during harvest should provide for hunger.

One more thing you must understand James, Do not approve of aimless dissipation of energy for labor.

The easiest way to make a slave out of a man is to give him what he wants and make sure he does not have it, and then you can be sure he will work for it the rest of his life.

When a man has gotten what he wants in life, he looks another way. This is how manipulative this life can be. But for you to secure yourself in life, you must hold something unique, or you will sure suffer a loss in the bargain.

If you never work, you are afraid you will starve, yet you work so hard for what you will never have enough.

Labor has its magnitude and direction to either good or evil. Your reward is already with you. If it is what you never desired, then discontinue the act before the next parcel arrives.

50

CONFLICTS

It is not an unusual thing to shed tears but it should be better done at the best times. At one time or the other in our lives, things do get out of our control and at times we consequently lose control of ourselves.

We can stop the things we never started just as we can start the things we can never stop.

People cry when unforeseen circumstances set in, and it is not a sign of weakness to express grieve.

> *Grief pumps excessive energy to your other person which has to be let loose*

through the eyes, hand, mouth or any organ of communication to free the soul before you can regain effective control of yourself.

That is that for grieve but do not confuse grief for pains.

Pains are direct impact of external or internal force on you and it is no good signal for tears.

> *It is a foolish thing to shed tears when in essence you should gather courage*

I approve of the philosophy of Sparta, "Never show your pain". There are circumstances that undeserved pains surround people of social connection to your affection and the banks of tears let loose its content.

There is no wisdom in indirect attack and

it is indeed a sign of weakness to attack a man from behind.

When things come to you straight, it is real and reality should only be faced not avoided. Crying does not take away reality and the pains continue unless you fight back. Sometimes men attack just to see you cry, do not give them that easy pleasure; if you refuse to blur your mind with the flood of tears, you will see your enemies clearly as they reveal themselves.

If you have scores to settle with a man, do not attack his wife or children. These ones are no alternative and they only bring grieve not pains. If you cannot attack the man in question, then let it be and go pleading for peace.

Tears are better shed in joy and courage summed in pain. Courage, James, for no man is stronger than you are but not every man you should launch attack.

Do not fight because of the weakness of your opponent, but fight enough to defend your integrity. Intelligent people take offensive position, the revenging side is at advantage, but wise people do not show their strength.

> *Do not follow an angry man to war, you might be committing suicide unawares; these angry people hardly see their way properly or come up with good reasons or strategies.*

There will always be temptations to serve your vengeance in the heat of provocation, but be careful, you never know how long the other took to plan the attack, and might still have some more tricks up his sleeves.

Vengeance is better served cold, and even if you are dead, do not be in a hurry to resurrect, you might not be strong enough for the next blow.

> *Combatance is no sign of reason and wars do not proceed form reasonable minds.*

War, it all began when the first weapon was fashioned, and will never end until all weapons have been destroyed.

War has only one soul, the weapon in your hand; if men had no weapons, none would go fighting. Destroy the weapons and the war will end.

> *No negotiation of peace will ever succeed as long as we are all deceived by the strength of our armory or the power of our strategies.*

There would have been no war in heaven if angels were not going about with swords.

And no conflict can ever be resolved as long as the parties persist on lies.

I used to think it is not good for men to have weapons, but when I discovered others who had theirs are becoming mad, I realized it is useless playing the weaker sect.

> *When I realized that men do not provoke a dangerous man for fear of getting hurt, then I counsel any wise man to appear dangerous without even if you are not so within.*

51

PURPOSE

Everything in the world is vanity. It is vanity to be born and vanity to die, but this is no excuse for not living your life. It is vanity to get what you will lose but this is no reason you should not struggle for the wealth that nature had bestowed. Everything in the world is meant for our utilization only to live it behind for the benefit of the next generation of people.

Wars and destruction is wickedness against nature for it mars the page of our time and leaves untold hardships for the next generation. We can only build on our successes not our destructions.

The world has not produced the population it cannot carter for but humans have obstructed the free circulation of resources. We call this the wickedness of man towards man but for what, when we will all die.

Humans rise and make claims even beyond their natural bounds yet none has ever resisted the blow of dead.

It is rear wisdom to understand the vanity of life

and those who do make perfect humans by it. I used to wonder when I see men and women hold sway to positions and things as if there will be no succession, and yet many of them did little or nothing to prepare the ground for the next generation.

Death in life and life in death has no meaning in it but promises uncertain. Perfect not because they escaped the fangs of death but because they managed their life as pilgrims that came and will go.

But only one thing is not vanity in your life, you! The reason you were born is not vanity, the purpose of your life is not vanity, but if you lose this, then you have got nothing.

> *Your soul feeds and is made fat by your purpose, and no man that loses his purpose will ever gain his soul.*

Life is so boring when you do not wake up each day with a goal in mind, with some worthy course to pursue unto accomplishment.

Today we rise and tomorrow we fall only to hold onto the foundation we laid while we were on top.

The life of man weighed on the scale, has nothing to show except the hope we have for hope.

Little things are what we make big and trivial things what we die for, but even this is vanity of the first order.

People who understand the vanity of life are never afraid of judgment nor punishment and not even death.

What is it to fear in judgment when you are just or punishment when you are guiltless and even death, when it is a necessary end for every living being on earth.

> *There is indeed nothing worth dying for, except the very purpose for which we are living.*

To struggle so hard over what you do not even need in life is foolishness of the first order.

But if you know the things you need in life and go only for these, then you will realize life is not as terrible as we make it to appear.

52

INSPIRATION

Inspiration is a rare ray that strikes the mind of man as proceeding from the beam of nature finding perfect disposition, and sparking to ignite the visitation of a chain of reactions towards the accomplishment of the non-existent perfection.

Because the beam is scattered as radiating from the fire of nature, with distinct rays that hold different missions, every person can be disposed to be inspire but each in and from distinct un-identical way to the other person.

We separate inspiration the precursor of good and branding instinct, the precursor of evil.

> *It is inspiration to begin that which is good, it is grace to continue in it and more a blessing to accomplish a purpose.*

Nothing discourages like failure!

Thus when you have been perfectly inspired, you must realize imperfect perception, poor preservation, limited means of communication and expression.

Big dreams will always come, but be wise! Break them into tiny bits and take them one bit at a time.

If you succeed in the bits, you will soon succeed in the whole.

Be careful of the power you have over yourself, less you fire a dream that would have hired you for life, and that, for a good pay.

In a seed is buried a mighty tree; if you grow it and do not abandon it to die, it can be there to feed you for a good part of your life.

Not all who start a project continue in it. Many people are open to too many rays due to the disposition of their mind consequent of non-directional trend of their thought.

A man is either thinking of a particular thing or he will be thinking of too many things, and this is the confusion of many. These ones may find themselves jumping from one project to the other without really spending time to see to the actualization of any of them.

To the man who does not know where he is going every way would look like the way

Other people are there who are too dull to reflect the ray of inspiration due to their myopic approach to life.

Unless you have the fuel of knowledge, you might not be ignited by the fire of inspiration. And even if you do, you might not burn for long.

Narrow mindedness may let inspirations suffer, thus, as soon as the fire is kindled, extinguished.

By grace, inspirations find footings to sprout and grow.

The grace may take the form of societal influence or the situation of things and yearnings, which is the support of the people and their readiness to accept your vision based on how it affects them, and your ability to restore the hope of a better future in their minds.

Paint your dream in bright colors, and never leave any stone unturned until you have a perfect sellable image.

Always remember that a good package can sell a poor content especially if it is not poison.

The more the people see, the less you will have to talk.

But it is possible for the good to perish from existence if nobody knows about it.

With inspiration and grace, it is even more a blessing to accomplish a mission in life.

Many people start things and others complete them.

If you started and have the opportunity of witnessing the fulfillment of your dream, count yourself blessed.

Be careful not to fumble along the line and never take undue advantage of the people.

> *As much as is in you, develop the habit of always giving your best to what you do, and someday you will come to abundance of riches.*

53

COMPETITION

Life is all about struggle to some attainment and you are the one to be crowned the best.

This does not come easily as you are not the only person that wants to wear the crown, but only the one that can bear the cross.

It is better when you know your fellow competitors but on many occasions, you seldom have the knowledge of your contenders.

> *Many people do not understand their position and thus are afraid of competition.*

Life is competition, there are more people for the scarce resources, more candidates for the few positions and it is getting worse by the day.

Look around, people are even scrambling over what they pay for, struggling to earn and struggling to buy. Now ask yourself, what you have, is it enough?

> *If you must get to where you want, then the knowledge of where you are is the first to be taken into consideration. Never forget the place and time you are in life, these are two important determinants of your success in destiny.*

Many more people are so afraid to face their real selves and thus cannot attempt to face others.

If you do not know your strength so well that you can be confident in it, then you are not fit to stand in the battle of life. You must understand that a man is an army and an army is the arms of the man commanding. A general who cannot hold his army together and direct them as a swordsman his sword is not fit to win battles.

Many people answer names that do not describe them and others accept titles that hang loosely over them.

Some people do not even have an epignosis of what they are called and you can be surprised seeing these ones displaying their thirty two at the sound of it.

> *Every power is open to opposition and every Kingdom prone to attack.*

People are carving out niches for themselves, creating for themselves kingdoms in specialties in order to be relevant to the world system.

If you cannot see your kingdom, then you will die as a slave in another man's kingdom.

There are vast territories undiscovered, discover one and rule, leaving an inheritance for your children.

A man learns on the trade, but no man struggles in his purpose.

> *Do not go about with a common skill, you will be living at the mercy of few people who pretend to like your face; but develop a rare talent and you can always get your worth and live large.*

We can spare ourselves the embarrassment of not being able to defend our titles by trekking only on grounds that we can protect ourselves.

James, do not accept the top before you climb to it for manners alone do not make the monk.

There is a deeper way than what you are seeing if you care to understand.

Those who accept positions beyond their strength explore all avenues and employ all forces not to be overcome for they in themselves know they cannot overcome any of their contenders.

You can run through if you can afford but do not jump steps as every step is unique and important. Never miss your lessons in life!

The top is for you and it is your position to get there, but do not sit on the throne yet until you are truly the King.

You are never thus, until you are safely thus.

You truly have a kingdom if you can make men pay tribute to you, this is the portion reserved for kings not stealing from public treasury, go beyond borders!

You cannot become a champion lying in your bedchamber; you have to win battles to be a true general.

54

CORRECTION

It is no sanity trying to change that which does not exist.

Salvation, they say, does not come before the acknowledgement of sinful position

It is piteous that the fool knows not his own foolishness.

A fool is like a closed tank and so full of his own self.

Where ignorance is bliss, it is folly really to be wise especially when you approach the awkwardness in a direct manner.

Go straight to open the tank and he will employ all the force that exists in him in resistance to your attempt. But if you want it open, throw a stone to trigger a reaction and before you know it, he will open and let loose its content.

No foolishness exists in the mind of the fool as far as he is concerned, but in an atom of wisdom, he will realize the emptiness of his bowl that grace may fill it to the brim. It is thus disheartening sometimes to realize that even what you were proud of, was a bundle of absurdity.

When a man has discovered his foolishness, he will become humble, gentle, fearful and shameful; but if he is arrogant, he will die in his foolishness.

Every man is entitled to his opinion but it is better to understand the opinions of others to see if they can justify your own.

There is one thing that makes a fool, the comfort he derives in his foolishness. You must always remember that a fool is very comfortable with his position, where it not so, he would have changed yesterday.

No man will trade off his comfort easily, just like the pupil of the eye, the more light you shone on it, the more tightly it closes.

Every fool hides under a cover, but if you are kind, find out and remove this cover from his head, as the sun touches his head, one day he will get wise and move away from his foolish stand.

If you remove the cover from the head of every fool, you will throw the whole world into a serious chaos because there are not many wise in this world, most of us are just hiding under a cover and tagging along.

You cannot tell a grown up man to leave the sun, simply remove the umbrella from his head.

However you may feel realizing your erroneous position, be happy within yourself that you have displaced a good amount of ignorance.

The human mind, if not filled with wisdom, fills itself with foolishness, but a wise mind contains some trace of imprudence.

It is indeed foolish to realize you are the wisest man

for by these you have deprived yourself of a good amount of wisdom.

No atom of water can enter a full cup undisputingly.

It is either displaced or it displaces another atom.

Wisdom does not seek the vacuum, but the dwelling place of ignorance.

In fact, there is no vacuum in nature. Even the abandoned caves are inhabited by demons.

Poverty becomes a safe haven for a man who lies about his occupation; even as he goes about doing nothing but trying to prove to everybody he is doing something.

Vain occupation is now a popular form of self-deception. These types, James, will never break from poverty.

55

GIVING

For everything you receive, is something expected of you. The most important thing in receiving is gratitude to the source of the goodness.

It is a law of nature that he who takes so much and does not give back a little, will soon find himself losing everything he thought he had accumulated.

> *No matter how miserly a man is, he will never fail to defecate, or has he forgotten that excreta is also a worthy possession?*

The river is always receiving from the stream, yet is not full, because it is always giving to the ocean.

The lake stinks because it receives from the sky and gives to none.

A receiver is a debtor for what he receives from nature or fellow humans.

Debts deprive the mind of peace and this is what it should be.

It is obvious, some people who receive do not have the worth to give in return and indeed

> *gifts should not be returned but given.*

There is always something you can do to show your appreciation of people's gesture towards you.

The word of thanks is sufficient from the poor and even greater than the gifts we receive if it comes from the mind.

Whoever defers the debt of gratitude or fails to acknowledge somebody's magnanimity has placed a log on the way to his warehouse.

Unless you remove this log, it can be almost impossible to get anything more from the source.

No matter how close you may feel the source is to you, do not be deceived to believing that he will understand, and there is nothing really to understand no matter how poor you may feel you are.

Nature expects that when you pluck from the ground, you return something to nurture and prepare the ground for the next time you come to pluck.

If you do all the plucking and no return, there will come a time you cannot get anything from nature no matter how hungry you may be begging.

In the harvest preserve a seed, and be sure to sow it on a fertile ground, or that may be the last harvest you ever have.

In the same vein, if a fellow human indebts you in one way, try and indebt him in another way.

Every person deserves and expects gratitude and you should not make yourself the all debtor.

There is a way you can indebt him, just try and find out and you will be happy you did and your mind will find some amount of respite.

56

SERVICE II

It is not an easy task to be a servant. Putting oneself into the service of another man is what many people cannot do though it is not below human dignity to do so. If you pray to be a good leader tomorrow, then you must put yourself to the service of a good leader. A leader who does not understand what it means to be a servant often end up as a tyrant that must be avoided or eliminated.

The master is not more important than the servant but the two must exist each having the welfare of the other in mind.

If a child is willing to serve you, accept him; if he despises all things for your service, honor him. If he serves you in sincerity, glorify him.

A lot of people who Lord themselves over others take pleasure in playing with the mind of those who have agreed to serve them.

I have this to say to every servant, civil, public or domestic that no master desires a servant with ambition.

While you are in the service of another man, you must learn to shelf your ambition, or this will only earn you unnecessary suspicion. But no matter how lowly your service, have a vision of yourself and work it every day of your life.

Work your dream with every strength that is left in you, and if you can choose who to serve, never bear a service that does not complement your dream.

My friend joined the military service yesterday because he believes that way he will gain access into the corridor of power, and would one day become president. That's a dream!

It is not easy to despise the pleasures and highly things to put yourself to serve a fellow human being even if the person in question is regarded as a halfwit. Even imbeciles many times refuse to bear service to a sane man in the community, and more, there is no good you can derive from an imbecile.

Any person who can serve you satisfactorily is an intelligent person, with full dignity, with streams of emotion and more the virtue of humility.

> *Before you treat your servant in an insensitive way, ask yourself how many people you yourself can serve?*

If you cannot humble yourself to go into the service of another man, why not respect the other that has accepted that virtue to your own good?

> *Yes, the call to service is heralded by wants and necessities, the pangs of hunger, the woes of poverty and the need for security; yet, it is a virtue to serve another man.*

There is more for you in people who have nothing than all that you have in yourself put together, even if it is one half of the world. The only way to get this is by reaching out to their needs, and you can get from them what you need to prosper above others.

If you can serve the better, why not try and see the difference that exists in the other person? You possibly were not born on the same day, in the same home, into the same environment nor receive the same training.

Do not withhold the glory of your servant for this does not make you the richer. A man who will not die in peace is one who cheats his servants out of their wages; he will never live to enjoy the loot.

Your riches come from the encouragement you give to those who work for you and you may not be as strong and dexterous as they are. If you treat your servant well, you can have him as a son at the end.

Do not give your servant in sincerity a cause to regret his sincerity, for you will never find any of sort again in your life time.

There is no sincere servant in a child of ambition. Sincerity and ambition do not dwell together in the same man.

Next time you are buying a fowl, check the head, if it is corrupted by ambition, it will certainly pluck out your eyes.

A man who cannot shelf his ambition in the place of his occupation is likely to steal from the corporation.
Be careful with a servant on a journey, he will leave sooner than expected if he can get his hands on your money.

If you find out what a woman wants, which you should find out for your good, make her wait for it; or the very moment she has got what she wants, it will be very difficult to make her stay.

57

HISTORY

Soldiers come and soldiers go but the army remains. Human intelligence come and depart but the world and humanity persist.

The best has not yet come, but the most important is the foundation that can sustain the height.

All these begin when men quickly forgot their joys and hung on to their pains; they talked of these a lot until it never left their minds.

From the age of primordial investigation to the age of knowledge, to the age of reason; the age of justice to the age of development, giving way to the age of deconstruction, knowledge makes way to knowledge and by counting one, we get to two.

We cannot take away the place of religion, the very bone of history. Be it the bone of contention or the soul of human affliction, it has done its harm and good.

But when hate and prejudice is being taught in the name of religion, what else can the world expect besides wars and destructions in the name of revolution.

If you look at it closely, virtually all the wars and destructions that have been perpetrated on the earth have been under one heading, "The just course"

Ignorance of history, it is said, is ignorance of oneself and nothing springs from nothing.

A better history to follow is of men who discovered their purpose early and followed same, for this is the same thing expected of every man.

The rest is the woes of men who wondered from their path to pierce themselves with many sorrows, fighting for things they never needed, and dying for things they never lived for.

You can never get wise in life following after the story of fools, the companionship of foolishness will transfer foolishness.

The reason for human succession is to link the new generations.

There can be no link without the aim of transfer and linking human generation means transferring what the former had gotten, discovered, to the next generation.

It is obvious many who received find it difficult to pass the knowledge to the next generation of people, and die with their knowledge dying with them.

You do not have what you cannot show no matter how fat it may be, hidden in you.

Whatever comes to your court, pass same to the next, this is what spices the game.

Whatever comes to you is consequent of precursors established by other minds. You may be the first to decode the signal that we call discovery, but you cannot claim its origin.

Everything we discover had its origin billions of years ago and many people have pondered over the picture, though; it never appeared to them as clear as it is to you.

Yours cannot be the best with time.

Human evolution is a continuous process, and a man is as refined as the tools used in working on him.

You are able to see because someone opened your eyes.

Keep a good record of the path and the struggle, somebody will get better by your findings.

Withholding the experiences we have had in life is why confusions still abound on earth.

If those who have found the light refuse to shine it, then everyone else will continue to grope about in darkness and confusion.

> *Every era in history has enough information to establish sufficient order in it,*

all hidden in the minds of the people living within.

James, you will never have the better part of wisdom unless you dispose of the former.

Over the ages, all through history, revelation has always come in degrees.

Keep looking and you will always come out better.

> *What you have found today is not the best, if you keep looking, you will discover there is always something better to search for.*

Knowledge my dear is infinite!

The higher you go, the better you become. But if you keep getting the wrong stuff, you will get worse any way.

Do not bother much about who receives, but give, even to anybody.

There is so much treasure buried in history, and the man who searches for these will come to many riches.

58

TOLERANCE

You know we are very different people just as you are different from every other person. You are unique in yourself, the very best of you, yet still, you can attain a better part of yourself.

Compare yourself to any person you feel is better than you are, and count for yourself the many infirmities you will discover in yourself. Though this test may prove positive to you, but the truth is that nobody is better than you are nor are you better than any other person no matter the defects you may obviously find in them.

So James,

> *always learn to bear with the defects of others conscious that you yourself have many infirmities that others bear with you.*

If you keep smelling rats everywhere, be very careful that you are not the very rat you have been looking for.

If only you can be patient with people for a while, you will soon realize that they are not what you thought them to be.

If you have been blinded by prejudice, you would hardly see the brightness of an angel standing before you.

> *If you become a victim of bad counsel and fake prophecies, you will soon view everyone around you with suspicion and yourself in frustration.*

But if something always smells, check your armpit; it might have become a soak away.

Forget about how much praise you receive in your before, do you know how much fault they find in your behind?

Those who are conscious of their own wrongs find it difficult to point at your own errors afraid you will uncover theirs in return.

He who points a finger at the other, it is said has his other four fingers pointing at him.

Social incompatibility is a discriminatory terminology,

though it applies in real situations due to the variance in our individual tolerance capacity.

There are no irreconcilable differences in life, what we have is only unforgiving spirit come to play, and men of little virtues insisting on the rights they do not even understand.

You cannot be perfect beyond all infirmities though every man is perfect within the bounds of his nature.

You cannot shift the bounds of nature no matter how much you try but if you focus your energy in polishing your potentials, you can be magnificently and exceedingly bright and glittering.

It is not as if you have done anything special, the glitters are inherent in the diamond though it might first appear a bunch of coal in unpolished state. But even with this there is a mark.

You cannot cut your nose to spite your face, and so do not expect it from others. But you can assist others to accept themselves as they are, by first accepting them and then explaining to them the prospects of their nature.

If you correct your inability to bear the defects of others today, you will keep a million eyes off your direction. But if you are always seeing problems in people, do not be surprised when you look closely, that you may be the very problem that needs to be solved, you could possibly have a bad eye.

59

JUDGMENT

With the measure you measure out to others, that it will be used, in measuring out to you, so says my book of religious piety.

> *With judgment we attain justice but it is grace, the sense of sound judgment.*

It is often thing we judge others and more often than usual we see only the bad side of the other person.

The good side of others is not easily subject to judgment except by nature, for we say it is self-manifest but it is not the way you understand. The truth is that it came from the other person not you.

You would want to be judged and rewarded if by crook or accident you committed the good act, but this is one injustice of man towards man since the days of Socrates. The wisdom of the poor is always despised, and the poor is hated even by his own family.

If you persevere in judging the standards of the other human, first put yourself on the scale. Whatever ratio you have of good and evil, use it to measure the other and divide it by the difference between you.

James, compare for yourself, the things you did to the things you ought to have done, the things you ought not to have done to the ones you did.

What then are the things you expect from others and how many of them do you have the hope of getting compared to yourself.

You have been given two ears and two eyes, but only one mouth so that you will learn to see and hear more, but always be sure you think before you talk.

How many of the things we criticize have we never fallen victim of at one time or the other?

And how many other wrong things have we done that others have never done before. **Some things a man does are just weaknesses; they are not equivalent to wickedness.**

Some of the things you find yourself doing is not who you are, you must endeavor to know yourself and get back on course.

This is the standard measure, your reading has to be different from mine simply because we are different people.

When you who have a sense of expectation fall a victim of so many flaws, what then do you expect from others who may not even know what you expect of them.

This is the bane of many and the reason we shout on others when in reality, we are worse than they are.

The standard is to judge with consideration, and be moderate with our expectations of others.

Even when you are tasking your servants, be gentle with a willing horse.

60

EXPECTATIONS II

A man's life starts from ignorance and grows on expectations. From the day a child starts school he has admiration of what he will like to be when he has graduated. Parents and the society have expectations of their children especially as it has to do with what they have put into their lives or so they feel.

Based on the grounds of expectations, we easily judge failures and successful children both at home and in the society.

Many of the people we brand failures are not really what we think but accepting the susceptibility to the forces of their nature, the environment and the rules of accomplishment.

It is a common mistake that pearls are expected from the vine ignoring the purpose of individual design according to given potentials, although it is not everybody that believes in destiny. It is wicked for any man to expect another person to live all his life fulfilling others wishes despite his desire for self-expression. No matter how you succeed with the tasks of others, you may never end up with a sense of fulfillment. It is always better to do your own things, and do it well.

The people we term successful in life only wear vague smiles
for within them exist bundles of failures and regrets.

You can be whatever you want to be, but you cannot be everything you would like to be.

Of all your aspirations, the world only expects you to be somebody, you!
One ill about expectations is that we often do not include some gab

for deviation due to unforeseen circumstances, but want it just the way the picture exists in our minds.

Expectation is good when it is applying to oneself for it sets a target that spurs you into action but when we apply it to others, we are bound to get ourselves into confusion and disappointments.

It is only the pilot that can tell what he encounters in the air, and only the sailor can tell the woes of the high sea; many times in life you end up with what you never bargained for in life.

James,

> *If you have been able to be what you had wanted to be in life, then expect the other to be exactly to your mind.*

Things do not come exactly the way we expect, though many people live perchance stance beyond their expectations.

If you are not prepared for the turn of events of your life, you may not prosper in it all the same.

Life is a cycle from day to night, from life to death full of ups and downs, all carrying with them their tokens of luck.

Nature operates on laws while humans operate on the combination of variable factors. In fact, unforeseen circumstances is one virus that plaques information corporations in my country and it can be disheartening tuning in for your favorite, only to hear it has been maimed by the infection.

> *Learn to be content with what you are, to be patient with the abilities of others and taking courage in the state of disappointment.*

Expectations are meant to set targets but keep some rooms for the forces of opposition. When you toss a coin in the air, expect the two sides, the head or the tail, and be ready to contain whichever side falls to you.

> *But miracles are born out of the womb of expectation in the place of worship under the enveloping presence of the spirit of the creator.*

Where there is infinite power to bring about possibilities as the nature of the Almighty is intercalated in holy intercourse with the spirit of the worshiper.

As God and man become one, God in man, and man with God, all things are possible.

The flip side of the coin still belongs to the coin.

61

CORRECTION II

Do not ever shy away from corrections no matter how and when it comes.

Absence of correction is the root of imperfection,

for the essence of knowledge is its power of self-correction.

By the act of correction, we institute a virtuous change of perception.

There is no seat of wisdom among men, nor is there such a place in human society.

Wisdom visits us from a distant town, and at times is already tired before it gets to our town.

Do not be so proud of what you buy from wisdom in your town, you never know what some other person bought before wisdom got to you. This is only the leftover; expect the original soon, probably from another man.

Change indeed is necessary in the life of man if at all man must accommodate the influx of revelatory signals that spontaneously trace his mind.

The series of human metamorphology from conception to decomposition is an example of how the life of man should be, though this is controlled by forces without man.

The series of constructions, deconstruction and reconstruction are necessary for change to occur if the very best is what we want to achieve.

The subject of change is not easy when it has to do with the human mind especially when anxieties fill his air and the present situation is not so problematic, might be due to the fact that he is inured to it.

Men get used to stinks, and the only way to make the change is take them to where the air is fresh and allow them to judge for themselves.

We are often anxious of the shame that may follow if we accept the correction but with the shame coming, the correction will not be established to institute a change and that, for the better. As you extend your knowledge and expand your understanding, you will find change and correction imminent and necessary.

Do not be emotional, it is the same to every man with better perception.

Men change the way they do things, and technology would not have survived without innovation with scientific discoveries.

James,

Anything that does you shame is meant to make you change.

This is one reason many people shy away from the truth about themselves and try to fight back any attempt to bring such to the open. I find men are more eager and ready to change others than they are to change themselves; we can easily announce that is who we are, but can hardly tolerate the same of others.

Don't ever be comfortable with whatever knowledge you have today, lest you find it hard to change for the better when you realize you were wrong. This is one problem with the champions of religion, they are too comfortable with the error they created, fearing a change will dedeify their personality. There is no supreme error, error is error, even if it stems from the gods.

To displace the wrong, you have to bring it to disgrace, for only in this will it be replaced by the right.

This is obviously one of the reasons you must tell the truth before the devil takes leave of you, but *those who conceal the truth pay tribute to undeserving hands.*

Those who are too stubborn to change to the right way always end their wasted years in regrets.

When shame comes, accept it for it would never have come if you had won a price.

62

LOVE II

Love is a spontaneous expression that is often blind to caution.

> *Not all the roses of love can be plucked within the ground reach,*

some lovers have to climb up the thorns of the tree to pluck the rose blossom. It is a nice sensation having a lover who can climb through such, just to make the mind of the other person.

Many loving hearts start right on the rough ground with nothing to hold unto. To these ones, hopes have to be built upon no hope and water has to be drawn from the rock.

When love happen this way, we easily term it 'True Love', even without paying much attention to what makes it true.

But if love hopes, then it does not hope for nothing, for hope is the tripod of love of many. And when this is dashed, such a love will summersault and pour out its content.

> *There is a secret in every loving heart that makes them stay right where they are. But some of them, just like many other secrets in life, are not worth knowing about.*

It is often said that love is long suffering; but why then do we find it following the direction of rich men?

However the variations in the objects of emotional infatuation, love is unique and identical to nothing than itself.

***When love does not express willingness in suffering, it is
rather rough for such to pitch a foundation***

Very little things make the mind grow yonder.

Unless the last stone is removed of the mount, the water will not flow
in the direction of the drill.

Marriages are made and many others as soon as consecrated
disintegrated. It is a nice thing to love and even better loving that which
is beautiful in itself.

However wild your emotions may be, a time of test will come and you
have to pass in order to be retained.

While you look unto the future in a love affair, the past is more
important if you have to reach there.

> ***A greater love is that which is shown to an imperfect person
> who you don't hope to change.***

Time heals the wounds of love but similar circumstances bring it back
in a more bitter way.

> ***It is grace to be forgiven but do not think it has been
> forgotten. The past will not help you to go forward, but it
> can certainly stop you from moving forward if you do not
> deal with it.***

If you do not have something outstanding which you built under
intense heat and pressure and which you can call the attention of your
love to when the winds of life blow, consider yourself a floater who will
soon be discarded. Memories protect the future, but everyman is capable
of adventure.

Do not dwell on the past so much lest you lose the future, love is a
burden that must be borne daily. Take stock of your trade and never run
short of supplies; daily you must fight for the love you have gotten.

When love is not given due attention, it will get sick and die eventually.

63

CHARITY III

Charity is a virtue that is built on human unconditional affection. Rich people often feel guilty of their inability to allow others have a share of their riches even when they blame the poor for not working enough to gain riches.

Many poor people who feel their poverty, wish they had enough that they may give to other poor people of the community, while many others swear if at all fortune will ever smile on them, nobody will ever smell their riches, feeling the insensitivity of the better placed individual to their plights. James, all these are human mental constructions and none has anything to do with charity.

Charity is unique in itself with its own rules.

Charity is an act of sacrifice.

Good sacrifices proceed from self-deprivation of what would have yielded better profit to you.

The principal rule of charity is that;

It is more dignified with your need than your spare.

The things that are of necessity to you is what will bless your act of charity if you can part with it.

Whatever you can afford to part is your spare but its idealistic to give that which you cannot afford to part with.

The ideal is a non-existent reality but the alternative is responding to the needs of others, be it with your need or your spare.

> *If you can live with this basic idea that you own nothing in this world, then someday, you will own everything.*

Charity is not a business, so be careful with what might be your interest, the magic of charity is that what you give away is what you have with you, the rest will go anyway.

If you go into charity with your spare, do not think you are the best because there are others who have struggled and parted with their need.

If you part with your life necessity, do not think you are the best because many others have parted with the very life they needed to enjoy their necessities.

If you can afford to part with your life as an act of charity, do not think you are the best because somebody gave you even the life you had and can afford to give it back to you.

Let the poor bless the rich and the rich also bless the poor.

> *The reason of the difference was to establish a game of exchange to spice the life we are living.*

Be wise with your possession, for you know not what evil shall befall the earth.

For any man who asks for the will of God in his life, it is that you do useful service to your fellow man, if not for any other reason, for the sake of God.

64

LOVE III

"Love your neighbor as yourself "is giant print in my book of religious piety. The more I realize the meaning of this statement, the more I love the philosophy as well as the philosopher. They call him Jesus Christ and I know he is a great man.

My neighbors were no real problem for me to solve, since I easily realized the whole globe is my neighborhood.

Since I never choose the place I find myself nor would I have rejected it if it were the other place, the real bugging question is, do I love myself?

I know I eat the type of food I like and do the best for myself but is this what the love of self consists? This is a question I cannot answer till today although I hope to answer it tomorrow.

The best answer I can find to these questions is what my book of religious piety put as the golden rule,

> *Do to no one what you would not like done to you. Also, do not to yourself what you would not like another person to do to you.*

To put it in a positive way, it means whatever we would like to be done to us, we should do just the same to others.

But if we wake up to the reality of the wreckage we have made of ourselves by our careless lives and choices, it does not mean the whole world should drown with us. It is only unfortunate that every dog that has gone mad in the name of religion wants to bite as many people as possible before it is beaten to death.

Love seeks the best for its lover and whoever seeks the best for himself is a lover of self and in the same manner, should extend that love to others by seeking the very best for them.

Love is humble, and cannot be found in the proud and boastful.

Love is kind, and cannot be found in the selfish and the wicked.

Love is gentle, and patient, and not the portion of fault finders and the judgmental.

James,

You will love others if you sincerely love yourself, but you will deprive the world if you love your flesh.

Love is a spiritual thing, given to them who want to attain higher goals, but ignorant men try unsuccessfully to change it to carnal instincts and fleshly lust, the portion of dead souls.

If I love myself, it should be sincere for from myself I can hide nothing.

The flesh is a servant of man, an invisible being.

Though the flesh of man we see, the very essence of man is what we cannot see.

Love of the flesh is negligence of its dignity for the flesh is no better than a servant.

This does not mean you should not love the servant but do not give to the servant, the love that is meant for the master.

It is the sacrifice of the flesh that makes the world fit for our stay, but if all humans should turn their love towards the flesh, labor will cease and we can imagine for ourselves the things that will follow. Until a man is willing to pay the price for a thing in life, the world will continue to languish in pains for it; sometimes it is necessary that a man should give his life so that salvation might come to many in the world.

65

PASSION

Nothing really satisfies though satisfaction is what we want from everything.

> *The thing we want and cannot get is what others use to deceive us.*

Miracles have its rule but it is the disorderly that seek it the most.

Miracles are borne out of the womb of expectation in the place of worship in his presence.

It is to defend his glory and not a show of power.

It is to correct the wrongs done by evil on His heritage.

Deception is an office in religion and the act of being deceived is a mark of simplicity with some elements of greed.

> *Passion deceives the heart with the promise of peace.*

Peace is what every man wants, but does cold come from fire?

Passion is as insatiable as Hades but will have as its first promise, a token of satisfaction.

It is the more you see, the less you like, the more reason the beautiful ones flock the streets at night under the cover of dark.

Lust will make you see what it wants you to see so you will allow it take what it wants to take.

> *Lust is one bloody merchant that trades on fake promises.*

The problem with many people is that their minds cannot fashion out for them when they are in emotional business to negotiate well, and they end up trading so much for nothing. You did not think you are in business, how come you are now counting the losses?

If only I have these one, I will never want again, who told you?

The beautiful ones are not yet born, it is often said, why then will the bird of beauty resign to the confinement of its nest.

> *Serve passion with a silver spoon, he demands a diamond platter for a dinning.*

There is something greater than diamond, but passion will make it the best for you until you get to it. You no sooner get to your object of infatuation than he shows you to another and the simple minds cannot but yield to the tune.

If men were to tell you the very truth about themselves, they would tell you that most of the things they fought and killed to acquire they found them so useless when they got to it to their regrets.

How quickly fashion fades, yet men are fashionable every day.

It is better with what you have at hand, but if this cannot satisfy you, do not think the other will satisfy you unless you will from there learn to be content.

If you plan to be content with the future imperfection, how will you reconcile the guilt of a former alternative?

You may choose to climb with passion to pluck the fruit of the apple that grows on the peak of the Mount Kilimanjaro.

> *The daughter of the King is not the best wife, nor the King the best of husbands. If you want to know the woes of marrying a king who is not in love, then listen to the tales of concubines.*

What you had chosen is the best yet until you can make it the better.

To tell you the whole truth, not all things in life are altogether good in themselves.

Most times, the good you see is what you make it, especially when you are dealing with men.

Do whatever you do for the good you see, but do not forget that the bad and the ugly are still in the same.

The reason love is strong at first sight is not that it will never grow weak, but that you may maintain its strength even in its weakness for the lifetime.

If you leave the weak for the strong, what would you do when that one grows weak?

You cannot continue this way for a lifetime unless you are the worst fool.

66

PASSION II

We are still on passion for it plays with the minds of men. It sweeps into man like the frontal wind in the Sahara blowing dusts up and down.

Passion does not want anything from man, it is in itself an integral part of man.

Passion is a swift prisoner of man and takes over the Kingship position at the slightest chance by disposition.

> *The wild wind of passion gives to no man an opportunity to contemplate on the state of his house*

until you reach the heart of the Atlantic.

You may often here people comment, what could possibly be a thing in the other person that this one wants to die for, if you are slow to realize you are saying it yourself.

You should not blame anybody on earth for leaving whatever or whoever the person loves because every single thing on earth was to be loved and hated.

That love is not seeing does not mean he is blind; he is only overwhelmed at the time by what he wanted to see and when he is done, he will see better, or perhaps, want to see that which he now wants to see.

> *I will advise you to seek joy in life, which comes with contentment, rather than happiness, for nothing lasts forever.*

When you realize the object of your passion is a disappointment, do not blame yourself so much for it had received the love it deserved and it serves you take your leave. When passion has taken you as far as the deep, it gives you an opportunity to realize where you are going, but not without an empty promise.

Many who die in a course at one time had a chance to make a retreat, but many surrender to fate whatever it maybe, and some could not figure out their doom.

> *By the means of a whorish woman, a man is reduced to a piece of bread, a strong man becomes a vegetable or worse. If you doubt this wisdom, learn a lesson from Samson.*

An adulteress is always seeking after a precious life to destroy it.

Be careful, for there are many of them moving up and down on our streets. When lust calls out to you, run, do not even reply!

Only the bold and brave in virtue choose to fall and swim back to destination while others simply resign to what fate holds for them the other side.

No distance is too far for anyone to make a retreat, but simple men will let the current finish its job.

If your house, as you realize along the line, will not contain the object of your emotional infatuation, what is the wisdom in pursuing it to the finish.

A Clothe that does not suit you does not suit you no matter how much you cut and join, and cut-and-join is not the same as the original.

Be bold enough to say no to a relationship that does not favor you no matter how far you had gone into it.

Do not allow people to deceive you that there is no way out, for

> *everything that has a way in, also has a way out.*

The best time to get out of it is now. Do not deceive yourself. Pretention in matters of passion only succeeds to build up a pressure that will someday cause you to explode, it could be a disaster!

*When you allow yourselves to be entangled in a problem
that only death can solve, then you can be sure someone will
certainly die someday.*

When passion makes you fall, do not confuse yourself thinking you
fall in-love; love does not make you fall, but love conquers all. It is only
lust, that makes a man fall right from the first man, and the result is always
a cataclysm!

*Do not be deceived by the beauty and the gifts; it is
a bait for your soul, the devil is never kind!*

67

LUST II

When I was a small boy, I used to go playing with Eros in his palace. I used to like him and indeed wanted to do anything that will keep us friends and this is neither true nor false for it did happen. For the time we were friends, I loved him until I realized who he was, a very smart employer. Pleasure is the second objective of life.

After any man has solved his basic problems, the next desire is to gain some amount of pleasure. And when this is far from reach, it can turn out a primary concern.

And anybody that has an idea of your problems, will try to proffer a solution, this is why we build corporations, to solve human problems.

We used to be playing with sex but we were different people I soon realized. I had a conscience in me but no trace of such was found on his face nor spelled from his act.

To me,

> *where lied the wisdom in spending time and money for a thing, only to regret at the point of doing.*

I never liked the game but he always told me there is something to gain and never permitted me to talk about the things I am already losing.

I realized early in life that there is no joy in sex when it is not the making of love. And worse, I see no pleasure in an act that is done with a guilty mind.

Peace of mind he always assured me of but,

where is the hope that peace will come when quilt is already knocking on the door.

By this time I no more liked the game but I liked my friend.

I thought I was going to make out something good talking to him concerning the game but he only explained that the game had been, ever before we were friends.

He made me understand the oldest corporation on earth is prostitution, the first to understand the strength of human sexual problems.

He told me the secret of good business, that as long as your business is there to solve recurrent human problems, then you will never run out of business.

He never stopped at this, but explored all avenues to intensify his lure with the consequence of changing me into his servant and he will enthrone himself the master by virtue of my serving.

One thought came to me one day, that I will be happier if I can resist at this point of intense drag and more that

he is a man who can resist the devil in his very plantation.

I simply went straight to him one day and said "no more". It was only then that I realized that upon all the noise he had been making, he had no strength but only capitalizing on my simplicity. He never told me what he will take from me but only what I will get from the game. But by the time I came back to my senses, I had lost almost everything I had. But I am happier because I am now free.

There is no destroyer of destinies than addiction, enslaving oneself to a known foe, loading the gun that is pointed at oneself.

68

LEADERSHIP

If you would ask me of the greatest animals in the forest, I would tell you they are the ants. They are but tiny animals yet build mighty hills that hide giant animals. It climbs with its food to the tallest tree and may choose to jump from the tallest height without breaking a single bone.

They never pass by a fellow in distress in a case of severe danger. They have no master between them but yet they maintain a high degree of order. James,

> *you have the choice to be whatever you want to be in life but be sure your house can contain your mass.*

A man is an entity in himself, and what law holds for him may have its holding in his human environment.

If the hands of human entity refuse the command to cut grass, the whole human society as a body will have a dysfunctional hand.

> *Leadership without empathy is equivalent to tyranny, a system of governance suitable for a man above sub-humans.*

As a leader, your faith will be tested in the course you champion one way or another.

> *Do not desert the course because crowds are not thronging you behind. You must be ready to make sacrifices, to fight alone on a course that many will come to enjoy.*

When you are going up in life, be careful you do not spend your little energy and scarce resources looking for men; when you make it to the top, men will come looking for you. The men that matter to your course, God himself will bring them your way if you trust in Him. Sometimes you must stand alone, and remain the last man standing.

Do not forget the rule that the more you give back to your source, the more you get back in return.

> *If you have the vision of being a King, start actualizing it by ruling yourself.*

You may think it is easy to rule yourself, but this will be proven when you start observing your personal rules.

Count for yourself the number of times you flout the rules you made for your own good with perfect understanding of the possible contributions of its observance to your life. Then imagine how many times the people will defy the laws you keep in the state, plus the fact that not all really understand the need to observe such laws.

Define a punishment for yourself each time you contravene your own rules and make sure yourself receives the full weight of its action, and then, count how many times or for how long you will stay without committing the same offense.

If you have an aching tooth, ask your tongue not to go there because each time it goes there it hurts, and see how many times the tongue will not go back there.

> *Do not think that other people are too different from yourself or too simple for you to be pushing around.*

You have to realize that human beings are good, and if few are bad, they do not represent the whole.

People do not obey the law because of the weight of offense, and many would not default if they had a better chance.

Lead as you would want to be led!

69

WARS

Fighting does not make you stronger nor do the resistant of the temptation to fight make you weaker.

It is good to know what you are fighting for, is it a want or a necessity.

Do not fight because of a want, for it is below your dignity, but in every necessity is the need to struggle.

Fighting may not be the best alternative in contention, but do not retrieve for an opposition.

If your opponent is very sure of himself, let him start the combat. War is human foolishness, but victory is great wisdom.

This is the connection of sanity to insanity for victory does not come without your fighting.

Do not condescend to fighting another man's war, except your life depends on it, for no king would start a foolish war if his children would be slaughtered at the war front. Every king you know will break down in tears when their children fall under the sword, but not the children of others.

Be sure that in fighting, you are not servicing the greed of some wicked men.

Being a great warrior does not consist only in knowing when best to fight, but more in knowing when best not to fight.

How would you feel if you were pushed to fight only to realize the other person does not want to fight you, not even by provocation?

It is wise to fight if you know you will win but the wise may choose not to fight if in case they may win.

Conditionals are not supposed to be confusionals, but precautionals.

It is safer not to fight if you are afraid you may loose and indeed not every wars are fit for fighting.

A general characteristic of any war is that it is an ill wind that blows no one any good, and wars only start and once they start, they never end, because the woes live on.

Great men, it is said, prefer to die by the sword, but not the ones in the hands of fools.

A man who fights with a child is below the dignity of a child, for that is what he is even struggling to attain, and same applies to a man of wisdom who goes to fight with fools.

If you must fight with a giant, prepare yourself for your burial but fight strong enough to destroy the very sword that is used for your execution. Remember, 'do not strike a fallen man'. The tiger does not show its claws until it is very close to the prey.

Any lion that goes about scaring its prey will certainly starve to death whatever the strength of its power.

For strength without cunning might end a mighty man in deep frustration.

leave the helpless man alone; the likes of the eagle and the tiger do not feed on carcasses, only vultures do!

If you find you are not strong enough, you may choose to kiss the ground.

Do not forget that if you loose and live, someday you may fight and win.

When the war is ended, be quick to deal with the army.

You cannot untrain a man that is trained for destruction.

If you intend to keep the army, then do not run out of battles.

When warriors do not have a better course to fight for, it is easy to take sides and begin to fight one another. Insurgency is an artificial creation of men greedy for war and whatever comes out of the chaos.

70

DEATH II

I am happy that human beings sometime die.

Death should be taken as an object of hope and caution, and not of fear and confusion.

How happy should man be realizing that no matter the trials and tribulations of this life, one day he will die and that ends it all.

Should a rich man not be happy dying in his riches, then he should live a donkey years to experience yet another round of poverty.

The best time to end a game is when the game wants to end but if you delay beyond this, a time will come when you will no longer want to play, yet the game will continue.

If you find yourself as a giant today, why should you not be happy that other giants died allowing the world to recognize that a person like you exist. Perhaps there were greater giants before you and they died to give you way, do you not consider it a mark of stupidity not to consider giving way to another person?

> *Those who never want to die cross the border of life before death appears.*

Nothing takes away natural laws, but because of our simplicity, deception has taken over the human race.

Why will I not tell you what you want to hear when I realize you are afraid of what is the truth.

A man's fear is the prophecy of his doom, and when he confesses it with his mouth, it becomes real and sure.

So many humans are so afraid of death that they contravene the law of life, and life cannot take it kindly with them.

There are only two things, life and death and they are real.

The thing that you go to for life had existed when every other human died. You go to it today, do you think your case is going to be an exception?

Nobody will destroy death except he that started life.

The fear of death is borne of ignorance, and the woes a matter of understanding; that which leaves to the great beyond is whole and complete in itself, and happier for the release unto a more beautiful world.

71

LOVE IV

Love is no careless affection no matter who, where and how it is cultivated.

Lovers see themselves as the best set of people and within the time taken to reconstruct their minds for the accommodation of each other, they have made up their mind if the worse comes to worse.

> *No matter what happens in the life of true lovers, there is always hope in one thing or the other.*

The hope of lovers may continue to be shifting from one thing to the other as soon as their object of hope becomes a disappointment.

At many times, hope may shift completely from the man or woman in question, to the product of their union, be they children. At many times too, what true minds need to let love be flowing is just the verbal reassurance of your existence for each other no matter the situation you may be finding yourself. Every woman in love has something in mind, and that is the prayer she prays every day, that her dreams come to pass.

> *Do not consider too much what to give for a hold when you are dealing with a loving heart, for it always finds for itself what to hold unto in the midst of nothingness.*

There is nothing like the best thing to give; just give what you have, and better what you do not yet have if only you can paint a picture that is real to the mind.

Love lives on pictures, the big future, the big dream; paint it with bright colors and you are the lover.

It is love to believe in my words even when you are disappointed by my acts.

If you were to ask me, I would tell you that 'love is scarce'. If you ever find one, hold on tight, for many are ever searching, but never finding.

If you need a perfect love, then you are certain to die without one.

True minds are often open because they do not want to see themselves parting.

When the expression of disappointment comes, this is the best part of your union, for the bearer of the complaint does not hate the defendant, but is only seeking a way to console herself that the worst has not yet happened.

My little advice to the captive of a nagging woman, tell her you love her even when she is spitting out fire and never return fire for fire.

> *Many nagging women do not mean the things they say, and when they start, they are bound to say so many things before they think.*

Nobody can give enough to deserve love, but true love can take from nothing and get started and going.

Do not tell a man why you love him, for this may be a sign of weakness on your part and it is the first point that he will attack when frictions occur.

You may tell him something close to what is real, but hid the real in the depth of the Atlantic, and let it reveal itself with time if it likes, but not through your mouth.

72

FRIENDSHIP II

Friends are not made for good times only and in fact, better friends are made in times of pain.

You will find more people want to share their pains than they will ever want to share their joys.

Your friend will want to be closer to you in their times of pains except when they are afraid their gestures will be misunderstood.

For those who want to bond, bonds made in times of pains last for a longer time. What fire binds together, it takes a greater fire to put asunder.

Friendship is an adventure, each wondering into the mind of the other to seek a hold for the fire that can burn for a considerable length of time.

Good friendships are not based on sufficient reasons, though each may find one trivial reason to give and those without the network may find it difficult to understand how that little can hold so close.

Many friends I know only live to chat away, having someone to talk to maybe the best gift they ever wanted. A better friend is one who has a positive impact on your person.

It is easy to see people make friends with tailors that they may sow their clothing, or with pastor that they may pray for them. Many others make friends with tappers that they may have an easy share of the tapped resource.

Going with a palm-wine tapper to his swamp can be an interesting experience and full of adventure. Watching him climb the palm may be were your desire is uplifted with all hopes that the best is about to drop.

It often drops for so many but at times catastrophe may set in to test your friendship.

Do not desert the tapper who falls – off the wine palm tree. You would have enjoyed the wine if he had been successful in the tapping.

A palm wine tapper gives life to the community of men, and may not really be interested in the proceeds that there may be. It has been known that a tapper that taps for the money will never give the best of the liquid; the better man is he who does it for the passion.

Those who do things just for the money will hardly have the kind of money they want, but those who put the best into what they do will have men begging to pay them their price.

A lot of friends go into adventures just to get their friendship going on. How do you expect these ones to feel when you desert them in their meeting with minor adversities?

We often hear friends say to each other, "I did this just for you," and it often may be a minor dishonorable act. You do not need to desert him even when he has become a knight of dishonor, but it may serve to have him understand he never needed to go that far.

Just give him a reason to believe he has never lost the very thing he had wanted to gain or these may start the decomposing part of his life time.

Just a little advice to a wayfarer: there are no friends anymore in the world; business and survival has taken the place of friendship; you can have gangs and fraternities, associates and accomplices, but be careful, there are no friends. If you can find one in a thousand, then you are the luckiest man, or maybe you are the only friend that there is.

73

RELIGION

Good things do not hide themselves though evil ones may wear the brows of grace. Many people allow themselves to be disturbed so much by the things that are not important to them.

All the things of life have their control.

The invisible things are controlled by the invisible one while the physical things are controlled by the physical force.

It was a state of mental laziness and swift aversion of difficult life puzzles that created the world of mysteries. As if that was not enough, we still have the mysteries of science that the things that have been known and felt are still unknowable to many is wonderment.

> *There are things that pertain to God, but to deny the realities of the known world is stupidity, not even in the name of religion, as especially any religion that does not open itself to investigative scrutiny may be an empty claim meant only to deceive.*

In the matters that pertain to our nation, let us rely on our constitution. But on the issues that pertain to life, let us rely on the verdict of God Almighty, the creator of all things, the owner of life.

Those in the light pay tribute to the master of light while those in darkness have the dark one as their master.

It is disheartening to see a married woman seek to live her life like a wayward one, and virtuous men try to live the lives of thieves.

If you are standing in the light, do not want too much to see those in the dark.

Seeing may corrupt your senses and there are many other reasons they are hidden from your vision.

If the ones in the dark were good enough for sight, they would not be hiding where they are.

However, do not be ignorant of the spirits, the good, the bad and the ugly, even the demons in abandoned caves.

Demons are seriously recruiting men to pervasion, and many are not aware of their evil all in the name of happiness.

Do not be emotional about a thing in this life, especially when you do not know the source.

As children behave to their parents who try to protect them from the forces without their compound, this is how man reacts to the natural protection they have from the forces that seek to destroy them.

Those in the light often want the place of the dark, thinking of it the best, while those in the dark, who have experienced the scourges of darkness, have the best part of their story to tell.

A common phenomenon of a top secret is that it is often an empty nonsense, and especially in secret societies, you find out there is no other big secret besides the people, and if they are very connected in the spirit, they have legions of demons in their bodies.

Whichever way you find yourself, seek the true knowledge of where you want to go, that you may not leave the best that has ever happened to you for the worse.

Opinions are no substitute for knowledge, even when it is a personal opinion of a very personal matter, or the overwhelming opinion of a public issue, wisdom seeks knowledge.

It may serve to declare another council of remiremont, but it will never present the best to humanity.

74

FAITH II

Many people venture into what they had earlier recognized as a mess.

> *The knowledge of an act is important to the actor, though*
> *ignorant actors are what we often see in real life,*

while the knowledgeable are too cautious to act out their scripts.

Where the talented have refused to act, charlatans have begun to act in their stead; butchers have taken over the theaters and fraudsters the pulpit.

Abomination is standing in the high place, and spiritual fornication and merchandizing is now a popular tradition. Hate, killings and extremism is a form of religious movement founded by the devil against his possible total defeat now and in eternity.

The matters of faith are things that are neither true nor false, but manipulations of the past to suit the possible future.

Truth is an Island, but falsehood has many brothers.

Where you stand is true as long as you are standing there unless you are told the evil that exists in your getting there. It is good that everyman choose just the best for himself, leaving no room for regrets.

The realization that your best is not the very best is a blessing to the person with the expectation of possible exploration of even the better that there may be.

> *You can be excused if you are not the best in the world, but*
> *there is no excuse for not being the best of you.*

Whatever you see in life affects your faith. When you have a big faith over little things, be careful of the things you have never known, or there might be a big problem when you know better.

Whatever choice you make is consequence of your knowledge, and this is what it should be, for anything out of this is below the dignity of any man.

Knowledge increases everyday and human vision of things become clearer with the realization of the in-built mechanism of your undertakings.

> *If you cannot own up to what you believe, then seek the knowledge of how you have been deceived.*

The best available definition of faith has been the substance of things hoped for, the evidence of things not yet seen, that he that said it can bring it to pass. And where does this confidence come from apart from the past, that what happened yesterday confirms it can be done tomorrow. The Word of God is God, and is surer than what any man can touch.

A true faith investigates the past to find out if there is a viable future as claimed, and so faith maybe about tomorrow, but it certainly comes from yesterday.

> *It is folly to trust in that which has not been tested, or to keep faith with error.*

It is possible that we make wrong choices due to our inadequate perception of the situation, might be due to our sophistication or probably how the things are presented to us. Many people believe God will do it, but they do not understand that he is already doing it simply because he is not following the way they wanted.

You will not understand the operations of God, until you understand he has the will power to decide how He does his things based on His infinite wisdom and unsearchable understanding.

God does not just do a thing; the Spirit of God executes the will of God.

The world is divided into realms even right where you are. There are things that exist that you cannot see, simply because of where you are.

Humans have learnt to manipulate the minds of others using fear and anxiety as advantage.

Sometimes unruly zest for the things beyond our capacity may make us vulnerable to deceit.

> *And you must understand that the best and easiest way to deceive a man is to make him deceive himself. That way he offers no resistance, and may even try to motivate you.*

Until you know who is working in you, you might not know who is working against you.

> *Though evil may wear the brows of grace, good is good and evil is evil,*

each carrying the consequence within and without the human self. Faith is pride not shame.

If faith does make you shame, seek the pride in your faith or think of a possible change. If it happens you have been deceived, it is human frailty to make mistakes but Divine virtue to correct them and be strong against further occurrences.

> *Your fanatical attachment to what is wrong can never make it right.*

Every man wants to please his God, whatever he conceives him to be. But any service rendered to God that does not benefit a man in need may not have God in it.

75

CONSCIENCE

The human conscience is the most powerful surveillance of human actions. If you consider anything can happen without your conscience's appraisal, it might be possible you were negligent of its rationalization.

Your conscience is the seat of justification of your act based on how the act appears to you, in comparison to the knowledge you had earlier had of the act. It serves man by giving him peace in acts in consonance with the preconception and establishing caution and anxiety in variation.

It is hard for man to get involved in an act that he is totally oblivious of its possible consequence and effect on his fellow human beings.

Even with these, things which are often wrong, which man gets involved, is almost always done amidst intense mental confusion with forces of urge and caution.

Although knowledge can be tagged to the source of evil, ignorance can never lay claim to good, having seen the much harm ignorance had wrought before knowledge brought salvation.

> *If your conscience confuses you on what to do, better seek counsel before you do the wrong.*

Amidst the urge and drag that may be, one's emotion will evaporate immediately the act is completed, which is the appearance of the first consequence of the series of actions. No matter how soon a man regrets, it is always too late for him.

Regret is corrosive to the state of confidence you have in yourself while aptitude is a sense of encouragement.

Human actions should not be subjected to probability for the effect of its consequence does not follow, but certain and very significant especially when carelessly done.

Probability is good with things whose effects are imaginative or a kind of non-existent reality but not a substantial act, and especially one which of the arms, pose a dangerous threat.

If you happen to find yourself at the scene of an act that you cannot comprehend, better stop acting at all, than act in any way.

It is better the offense of omission than that of an ignorant act. Knowledge might be expensive, but ignorance is even ten times more.

Knowing when not to act in itself is a strong virtue.

76

CONSCIENCE II

You may be ashamed of yourself, it is a good signal calling for a change of character but do not ever be afraid of yourself that you tend to avert.

The knowledge of yourself is very important so that you can manage your affairs, knowing the things that are beneficial to you, and the ones which may not yield a good aftermath, and try as much as you can to avoid them. There are many choices unto the man that does not know the right thing, but the moment you know the right path of life, you have only two choices, the right and wrong.

> *A man's righteousness is nothing more than seeking out that which is the right thing to do according to the time and appointment of purpose and following after it to do it.*

It is no sane thing keeping bundles of goods that do not have any prospect with regards to you, either in the distant or near future. There is no better way to prepare for tomorrow than to make the best use of today.

Not everything that come our way were meant for us as an end, but some were meant to strike us as means to an end, and thus absorbing this type of radiation into ourselves are almost useless to us.

> *Discrimination is an important character in a great mind, the one that understands the importance of higher goals.*

Disposition of useless things is a good development, for it allows room for the better things to come our way. But in doing this, we ought to be the most careful, less we dispose of even the things we needed most.

One problem with conscience is that at a time, it will appear to be fighting against us getting what appeals to us, it may even appear as an enemy of our pleasure, happiness and progress, and these it does as the only friend that desires for you only true happiness. **The last friend that will leave a sane man is conscience, the moment it is gone, madness begins.**

Remember Eve, if she had listened to her conscience, she wouldn't have eaten of the fruit, though it was pleasant.

A true love does not smile at her lover in the wrong. Conscience is one nagging wife you cannot divorce.

You cannot have a good conscience if you are plagued with poor knowledge and low understanding.

It is not good to dispose an old friend for a new one that you expect, though one may be told off if the two cannot be accommodated at the same time.

> *You may sell off all that you have but your conscience; it is the only thing that makes your being human.*

There is a marked difference between temporal things and human basic necessities.

The things that people often sell their conscience for is often, if not always, the trivial things of life. The most popular amongst these things is money, the root of all evil it is often called.

People who sell their consciences are more like animals, ruled by instinct. Just as animals, they are easily trapped by adversities no matter how strong they may feel, being void of cautious engagements.

> *Conscience is like a dash board of a ride or the cockpit of a jet plane, you do not switch it off simply because it is warning you of your dangerous maneuvers, and if you do, you will likely not make it far.*

Conscience was not built to praise, but to direct.

But you can do little about men devoid of knowledge, you can never build their conscience beyond their understanding.

Although the absolute loss of conscience is non-existent,

a gross level of neglect is worse than not having a conscience at all.

The man who fights against his good conscience fights against his future. This is not a kind of battle any man should desire.

77

SALVATION

In all things, I pay a little respect to the dark that gives definition to the light, and the light, whose creativity gave rise to the beautiful ones.

The beautiful ones are not yet born, it is often said, but the ugly ones no more exist.

The present state of man is sufficient for today, but may not meet the needs of tomorrow unless a little is added to it overnight.

No tangible change can occur in life without sacrifices.

The greater the change you want to see, the greater the sacrifices you have to make. Sacrifices fuel the process of any visible change, of status as well as momentum.

> *A human belonging is not as important as the means of obtaining, nor is salvation more important than the lamb of sacrifice.*

There cannot be a true spiritual salvation without a total and complete remission of sins, the very cause of human damnation.

The man that denies the place of salvation is likely that which thinks he is too buried in sins to be forgiven or which thinks he is too involved to come out in total repentance.

It is often seen that people no sooner attain the better part of their life situation than they forget how they got there.

You need enormous sacrifices to scale the heights, and only a simple folly to fall from grace.

Nothing lasts forever, and whatever you have today may never be there tomorrow, no matter how necessary they might be to your survival.

James, when I contemplate on the content of my little book of religious piety, I find it hard to believe that a man like me had the mind to die for my own sins, and that,

the first to do such in sanctity.

I have tested him and found that he works for me and because of this I am happy that I have a faith. It is my prayer that

the beautiful things of this life does not define my faith without mention of the cross.

For which benefit I am free from sin to live in righteousness, free from bondage into service, and from poverty to enjoy true riches that does not come with woes and sorrows.

A better rest from work is to engage in a work of little or no duress but better remuneration, but total rest from work is dead to the physical world.

While we exalt the glory of the crown, it is pertinent to keep the cross we bore to deserve the crown in mind.

The crown may fade but with the cross, we can fight for another crown, although it is even better to fight for that crown that will never fade.

There is this one thing about wisdom; you are wiser in your eyes when you haven't any.

Real wise men hardly face themselves.

If you were some of those wise guys like me, you would probably feel you do not need school or good grades to make it in life, just try the labor market and see.

And for those of us who really do not think we need a crown, wait until you drop the flesh, the spirit will tell you the truth. You must understand that the spirit world is as tangible to the spirits just as you stand on earth under gravity.

Do whatever you like with the gift, but do not forget the giver, he is the ultimate.

78

CONFRATERNITY

There is one simplicity I have observed amongst the youngsters of the generation, and this is ingenuity.

Every person is unique and sufficient to manage his own affairs, leaving the things beyond his strength to circumstances.

Two is companion it is said, but three is crowd and none do we need when it has to do with things strictly for our strength. There is one thing I do not like myself and do not know how many people do hate it the way I do, but feel these ones are many. What I am talking about is what we like to term "confraternity." I like to talk when it is time to talk, and too, to talk like myself.

> *There is no brother or friend in destiny, a helper is for a*
> *time and you have to move on to the next.*

You must not rest on the stairway of life; you either move up to the top or go down to the mass.

It is nonsense for a free man to be bound by laws given by a fellow who does not have your interest at heart. You must be careful the way you subject yourself to unknown authority of confraternity, you will hardly be smarter than those who had gone ahead of you.

> *They are cowards, who seek peers to overcome fears; there*
> *is not a single brave man in a band wagon.*

At times, it may not be fears but sheer anxiety.

Any foundation that contains human element is a porous foundation, and cannot sustain a great height, it will crack and crumble. There is no true foundation in life without true knowledge, the chances that work today may give in to chances tomorrow.

The best that humanity has created is a broken defense system, what trust then can be in your fellow man.

You are what you are and can never be what you are not, until you can afford to be.

Allowing people to influence the way you do your own things is below your dignity, and people who live below their dignity should be ashamed of themselves.

Your peers often think at the same level as you are, and what good do you think you can gain from people subject to the same emotions as you are?

Anything that stands in life, stands upon something.

Watch what you are standing upon and be sure it is not a dead trap. Great heights make greater falls.

If you are strong enough, then fight a course, but if not, do not open up for a blast.

The type of fear that exists in you, exist in your peer and do not expect that when you are gone, he will stand and fight in your place.

A man must overcome his fears to be brave, and there will always be something out there to be afraid of as long as you are alive. Refusal to fear what you should fear in life is foolishness, you cannot improve you strength with a broken neck.

Your peers may escort you to the stream, they do not often follow you to swim.

When you plan anything in this life, only plan with what you have and not what you expect; whatever is not in your hand may not come to you when you need it.

When anxieties are exchanged, vandalism may ensue. If you do not want disappointment and frustration to eat you up, then plan your life like there is nobody out there for you to depend on.

The best advice I can give you right now is to believe in God, and do not be afraid.

Do not be a fool for God is not a companion of fools.

Even if the world is coming down, simply step aside and let God have His way.

This world has an owner! Only God can blow the final whistle!

79

CHOICE II

It is no sign of right thinking roaming about seeking greener pastures when you can in fact develop one even at your very backyard.

The age of shifting cultivation is far gone and even that of crop rotation, leading into the age of artificial fertilization, representing human responsibility for his action and in the reversal of its effect.

What you have at hand can make the best if you put in a little effort to make it better, but it is unfortunate that the thoughts of many do not trace this direction.

But you can be a different person, thinking and acting in a different way altogether.

> *When you desert your dirty environment, this does not make you clean yourself.*

It is a real dirty human being who cannot make clean out of dirtiness.

The corruption in our country is human responsibility, and is human beings that will reverse the situation.

Real men do not trade blames or shift responsibilities rather they solve problems and make sure they are solved.

One day, you will realize that the primary objective of life is service, solving problems, yours and those of other people. Helping people solve their problems is the primary objective of life and vocation, and when you can add some fancy and pleasure to it, you become an expert.

The world is full of problems, and solving them is good business for all human beings. No person can solve a problem forever except God Almighty, any other who claims to do that will be deceiving others.

> *Almost all the problems you solve today will need a solution tomorrow; and so anybody that is in the business of solving problems will never run out of business.*

The only big thing I have seen about an expatriate is that they come from another country, but within are better hands without the needed chances.

You may choose to run away from it in your youth, when you would have championed your youthful creativity to changing the situation, only to come back into it at your old age when you can no more carter for yourself. Even a day will be enough to pay you all the services you had deprived your nation, even if it is your corpse that will kiss your motherland again.

It is even a greater disgrace accepting to be buried in a foreign land because of the corrupt state of your country.

> *The ability to clean linens is more virtuous than clean linens themselves. Any linen can be stained but not all stains can be removed.*

If then you can remove stains, count yourself a superman.

When you learn to clean your room, dirt will leave the bounds of your domain.

The clean things you seek were not born same, some people labored to place it at its state even without an example to emulate. You now have them for a model, why should you not do the better?

> *Nature sends you precious gifts in dirty sacks; diamond, gold, and precious metals in muddy earth, and every good gift endowed in an imperfect man.*

You may not know how many precious talents you may discover, if only you care to dig into your dirty self and purify its content.

How rich our world would be if only men were properly refined!

I cry for my country, where materialism has blinded our leaders to reality; that nobody gets rich by stealing no matter the volumes.

True riches can only come from the sacrifices we make to bring about development; but when one man steals, everyone gets poor.

But one man's ingenuity brings about many people's prosperity.

When a man comes to a pond of water in the desert, a fool washes his face and feet and keeps moving, but the wise man will build a city around it and live happily.

You cannot get everything from one thing; know what informs your decision and choices in life. And when you have found what you wanted, stick to it and be satisfied with what you have got.

Know what you want in something and go for just that; and when you have it with you, move on to the next.

It is only a fool who plucks an unripe coconut for its life giving water, and after he had gotten that, complains he found no flesh in it.

Until a man knows exactly what he wants, he will always be confused about his choices and decisions in life. You must first know what you live for, then you will better know what to go for in life.

80

POLITICS

One thing I fear about human beings is the offices they bear and their equivocal way of speaking.

> *A sincere man of our generation is one too simple to understand the office of cosmetism.*

Take a man for his word and live a life of regrets.

Man is truly a political animal if the politicking in the animal is lies and deceit.

I tell you the brand new one in town, that politics as governance is not common sense, but a game of strategies. People are always ready to take sides, whatever betters their chances in the game. The age of ideologies is giving way, because material gains have taken the place of faith.

This is why the good often end up not being chosen because they think being good is good enough!

The world is ruled and controlled by powers.

> *You need power to do good, you also need power to accomplish evil. You can never bring about either good or evil without the requisite power backings.*

This is where the good miss it, they feel because they want to do good they can simply wake up and do it.

This is not so; you need power to do anything, physical or spiritual, good or evil. Even Jesus Christ had to wait until God anointed him with the Holy Ghost and power, then he went about doing good. He also told his disciples to wait first until they are endued with power from on high.

I am telling you the same today, seek power first or you are likely to fail whatever it is you embark upon.

James, nothing will move from its place or state until power is applied; be it physical or spiritual.

There are no better sources of power than sacrifices of some sort. Find out what you need to sacrifice for what you want and do it quickly before circumstances change the price tag.

I tell you one thing about a strategist, he is not the man with the best touch, but one who rigs the game in a way that makes you clap for him it has been said.

Power is the best strategy for victory.

Evil has learnt to put on the veil of grace and grace is too shy to show itself because of evil domination.

Every right thinking man has got to look at things twice before approving of them, for many have other forms lurking behind their form and many other uses hidden behind their use.

I have learnt perchance stance to be more afraid of the friends I do not know than the enemies that I know.

James,

it is better to bark and kiss than to smile and bite.

This is one reason I prefer my father to my girlfriend.

My father may be as charged as the bull only to handle you as a lamb, but my girl will smile like Venus but the dentition of Lucifer. Open teeth bite deeper than griming faces.

I just remember what the grass cutter said to the hunter. He said, "Hello Mr. Hunter, when you come into this bush, you have got to get one thing straight. If you are looking for antelope to shoot, just be shouting at antelopes straight, not making confusing sounds. If you shout straight 'antelopes', we grass cutters will have peace of mind walking without fear of being shot even when you are not looking for us".

It is good to be sincere going straight to what you mean.

Confusing messages as well as obscured ones are very destructive.

If you are out to bite, it would serve but if to kiss, just try a smile. You will save the world this way and restore hope to some amicophobic chaps.

My pity goes to that country where public office is more of a place for common thieves.

The limitation of human knowledge is the bane of popular choice. Even this knowledge can be extended with proper investigation. But what can you do about a people who know about a thief and still approve of him?

A real man is a bundle of good and evil, he is the best man in the right places, and can also turn out the worst man in the wrong places.

Never be pushed hard to a corner in life, when circumstances have changed, a man is likely to change with it. No man can be too certain of what he will do in a tight situation.

Any man can be a criminal given the right circumstances.

Human beings are like metals, they all claim to be strong and do not bend under the same pressure. But if heated strongly enough, they are all likely to bend or break.

81

CHOICE III

First experience is often a harsh experience especially when it has to do with what will bring you good.

"No pain, no gain", is a cliché of competitions.

Things do not reduce from their level unless you reduce them or nature takes pity on it, but it is even pertinent you take to the path of endurance.

The human system is responsive to the stresses and strains that come our way every passing day.

The more often these come our way, the more our bodies are quick in responding to their effect. I hate observations that come from books, real pain must touch on the skin, and these the man can explain.

What cannot be cured, it is often said, must be endured and sometimes what will be cured.

There is no perfect knowledge or understanding on earth and so no perfect choices.

> *Lack of knowledge of what will be tomorrow is common to men of all ages, and there is a revelation for every generation; life is not a straight course.*

Preparation, it is often said, is the soul of success and the secret of good preparation is regular practice no matter the rigors that there may be.

Prepare for what you expect in life, and more for what you do not expect; do not be taken unawares, this is where many strong fall.

> *What tastes bitter, when often, becomes sweeter.*

You will not make it far in life if you keep living a life of denial, denying responsibility and changing course at every appearance or sign of pain or danger.

> *You are where you are today because of the choices you made yesterday, and you are responsible for those choices no matter what may have prompted you. You had the choice to resist but you did not.*

To make it worse, you are still going to be what you would not like tomorrow except you take a stand today.

Every road has some signs of the possible dangers ahead, but not all of them mean you should turn around.

There are certain risks you must take in life in order to distinguish yourself, but you must examine the game to know its worth.

Even what you are facing at the time can be the sweetest experience you can ever have in your life time if only you try to explore the apt perspective of it through frequent manipulation.

The simple things we have around were some difficult things, even too difficult than what you have, but some people devoted themselves to it, changing it to the form we now enjoy.

The blessing of subduction is what every man has been given but not so many can develop upon.

But James, you can be very different on this issue, you can make it the easiest thing for any man if only you try. Everything is possible for all who try their very best.

> *Get it into your thick skull that success is a commodity; and like any other commodity in the market place, it is only meant to be enjoyed by those who can pay the price or have others pay for them. As the prices of other commodities go up, so is the price of success.*

The problem you see today will be easy tomorrow because somebody is working on it. But then, it will become difficult for you because other problems will come around.

82

KNOWLEDGE III

Knowledge is the best thing that happened to man, though it gave name to good and evil.

A complete form of knowledge is black and white, black for evil and the white for good.

> *The knowledge of all good does not define good neither does the knowledge of all evil give any description to evil.*

Getting knowledge will always appear as a waste of time, but later, you will realize you save so much time, energy and resources having the right knowledge in you in good time.

Everything that has advantages, it is said, always has their own disadvantages though some may be slow to realize. Every good drug has a bad side effect, but the seller may not put it on the pack because they want you to buy.

The art of informing the masses of the prevalent evil of the society is more often than not the mutilating factor of innocent minds.

Be this as it may, ignorance is not a better choice to make.

The knowledge of poison keeps man far away from it, but it is the first thing that comes to his mind when in distress or the spirit of Lucifer takes possession of him.

> *A good knowledge of war gave way to defense but good tactics of defense push many into war.*

Knowledge is a two directional wind; it either blows you to the right or to the left.

By knowledge, man accepted responsibility for his action and ability to make it worse or better.

The worse part of all these is when you know not what you think you know, and worse still you know one thing in place of the other and you are out to defend what you know, you want everybody to know that you know and you want to show it and then realize you did not know what you thought you knew.

But if you do not realize, someone pays for it, the innocent goes to jail, even the world beyond.

You don't only pay for your actions; you pay for inactions as well.

But in all these confusions caused by the wind of knowledge, there is a solution that can be trusted.

If you have an anchorage, you can make the choice of direction.

It is not the best thing following confusion, but a little sticking to some source of strength will make the truth of the situation.

Sometimes it could be better to be rooted in a place you do not like, than to be blown by the wind to a place you do not know.

He who holds on for some time will know which direction is good and which is evil, making his choice according to his mind which of the two directions to follow.

If you cannot make out the way, it is enough reason you have not waited enough.

Tell me what time has not proven? Time is a great revealer of secrets and the frustration of falsehood.

Give truth a little time and it will come to limelight, but tell falsehood to wait and it will run into desperation.

So many things in this life will come needing immediate attention, but you must understand that this is one of the tricks of the conman, even the devil, take your time!

But come to think of time itself, that deceiver! You wait for it all the while yet it passes you by without your knowing.

Don't be deceived, the best place for time to be is yards behind; don't wait for it, always move ahead or you will spend the rest of your life running after it without ever catching up. Let time be running after you if it likes.

Time is always in a hurry, but so patient that the future will never struggle with the present no matter how close ten is to eleven.

A little more time will make things clear.

> *Man alone does not make his society; the society of man makes man. Give anything a little time, and you will discover in it what you thought was never there.*

You are not alone in this, hold on and you will see many like yourself. They are afraid they know nothing, so they must prove they know something, this is the confusion.

When a man is afraid that he is a nobody, he can do anything to prove he is somebody.

83

BUSINESS

He is not a man, whom all his actions are dictated by the forces without him.

You can keep the same law but in a way that suits you and not necessarily as it is generally expected.

> *Whoever knows what is good for him has the choice to do so, the same with he who can afford to do evil for good.*

Whatever profits a man let him do it, whatever makes him happy also. But in all of it, let him consider how long it will last.

James, whoever lives for himself, lives for nothing; but he that lives for others will live forever. There is always more for the sower!

Life begins when you see the need in another person or people and begin to fill it.

> *If you cannot see a problem to solve in life, then you are living a life of vain occupation. Do not just do what others do to earn a living, look around for a problem that others cannot solve, then develop the solution and put a price tag.*

You better watch your business! If it is all about you, you will soon be frustrated beyond consolation; this is where selfish people commit suicide when they meet the crossroad of vanity. I know of presidents who at some point in their lives after they leave power went bankrupt, only surviving on the goodwill of their few friends they once assisted, we all crash someday.

A man has to venture into things so that he will not have to regret even the best part of his life.

Whatever your hand finds to do, do it with all joy and gladness and all the power in you; and in righteousness, expect the blessing of God upon the works of your hands.

Those things which yield profit and good with him and others, these are the things that a man should learn to be doing.

> *This whole world is one big market. You have to gather in the morning what you intend to sell in the afternoon in goods and services; in the evening you will go home counting your gains and losses.*

You will not make any money except someone comes around to buy what you have to sell.

Be known for what you do and be sure your customers are satisfied and always come back to buy more. An unknown good will never be of any benefit to any man.

Life is simple when you know the principles and follow same.

Some profits are as soon as gotten lost, and the same applies to the kind of happiness we may derive from our works.

Many other profits have no profit in them, and are more destructive than the losses we may have been feeling.

One more thing, watch out for decay! When you steal and pile, will they decay?

When a man grows out of proportion, he becomes a burden he will have to carry for the rest of his life. Wise ones throw the burden to others and resign unto pleasure.

You need a thicker skin for a bigger size or some others will take out chunks to feed without your being aware.

It is never easy to cope with grass after a good time of grace.

The way we manage the grass may plunge us into grace and the way we may be acting in our state of grace may tend to reduce us to the grass.

Do not be over infatuated by the position that you find yourself in life, that you forget how you got there or how you can sustain yourself there.

Those who allow grace to climb their heads no sooner find themselves back in grass with the masses, but whoever respects the very minds that appointed him into grace and deals with them with respect, may be maintained in grace for a life time.

Mark you that by the time you return to the grass, the grass will never be the same as you left. This time, it will be so rough and unbearable and almost all will seem to be carrying thorns on their blades.

There is business success, a corporate success as well as individual success. There are those who swim in the euphoria of corporate success even when they little contribute and once disengaged, they crash beyond repairs. Whatever your career in life, you must have a marketable skill, and know how to sell same for personal coins.

Although corporate success is good, I see a truly successful man in the one who can fight his way through even when he is standing alone.

While you are shielded by another man's canopy, save enough to buy your own should that be taken away unawares.

84

SEX II

Some of the gains that man receive should better have been losses for him if he had a little time to contemplate the essence. The fact is not of no time, but that we refuse to carve out a little time along the line to think of where we are going and what we possibly want to get from there.

> *It is foolish to accept a bag of rice for dinner when your pot can accommodate only a cup.*

Sex is one human business that has survived the times despite the intensity of harm it is causing to humanity.

The reason of its proliferation does not consist in the desecration, but the curiosity of humans to derive sacred grace from a non-secretive act.

The only time humanity will kill sexual immorality is when they completely remove the elements of pleasure from it.

The worse happens when man has not many other option of obtaining his sensual pleasures, he resolves to sex, the only available option.

You cannot stop a young man from sexual pleasure when he has not many other options. When he is through with his day problems, the next thing in mind is some form of pleasure.

The worse is the man with no problems to solve, but enough currency to buy pleasure, and there is none that he knows of in his locality but sex and drugs.

> *Pleasure is a base instinct that fights against spiritual living.*

Sex education or no sex education is not important but the consciousness of every human person of the gain he hopes to derive from his labor, either as an end in itself, or as a means to an end. When a man cannot find a better goal to pursue, it is going to be difficult for such to remove his attention from what he has at hand.

The real gain we have in sex does not consist in the emotional release, but immediately after this forward.

For the careful wayfarer, sex is one pleasure that demons desire the most, yet have no bodies to actualize it by themselves; the only way out is to use the bodies of men, those who are careless enough to let them in, and even when they have been turned to bitches, they care not to realized something is wrong.

But James,

> *I will rather choose to die for a plate of rice that gives me stomach satisfaction than sex that laid my soul and body with burden.*

Burdens are good as means to an end but the worse that can happen to man as an end in itself.

Sex is beautiful in its time and for every right reason, but overindulgence in sex weakens the mind, the will and spiritual resolve.

If you have the capacity to contain the effect of your act, it is the right thing to do if devoid of uncertainty and any less a sign of caution.

He who cannot think should be made to understand and he who does understand should do no imbecile act.

Plaguing of self with emotional satisfaction

And depriving of self of release from burden is all a matter of volition. The ignorant should not act nor should the informed display incipient actualization.

What comes after what you get is as important as what you get at the end of action. Treating the important as unimportant and the unimportant as important is all but self-destruction.

It is good to live the moment only if it all ends here. But sexual urge is more of an emotional blackmailer, it is never satisfied, it will still come back for more even if it tells you this is the last time.

Watch that trap. The moment you like it, you will always want it even from the wrong sources.

Any kind of pleasure is capable of forming an addiction in the victim.

Open shame is the potent cure to secret pleasure.

85

LIGHT

Do not mix immiscible things unless you make the effort to know why they refuse naturally to mix.

Incompatible things should not be forced together though this should not apply to man.

There is no boundary between light and darkness unless you place a division.

Though darkness always owe light a respect and pays same by shifting, light should not push darkness to the wall.

Right from the time of John the Baptist, the kingdom of God suffers violence, and the violent takes it by force.

I see good people fail, and I asked why? Then I understand that the good fail because they think that things will just fall into their laps simply because they are good.

But is he a good man who does nothing in this militant world? Is he a good soldier who fires no bullet in the war front?

The evil know you won't give them except they fight their way and they have been fighting and getting; what is the good doing?

Though the children of light mix with those of darkness, light is unique as much as darkness is overwhelming.

Two bulls, it is said, cannot drink from the same bucket at the same time for fear of locking horns.

The elephants can exist as well as the grass but when they go into fight, the grass is at risk.

When you choose to invite the elephant and the hippo to a dinner, be there to separate them when they are fighting.

The Divine exist as well as the evil but when you choose to invite the two to your temple, what do you want to be your portion?

You can safely be an evil man as you can safely be a good man, but do not try to be this as well as that.

There are many secret plans, but no secret acts on earth.

The act done in the secret, will always find result in the open; and those who follow the lead, always get to the root.

Every secret act under the sun, is an open scandal in the spirit realm.

The good does not beg to stay nor does evil need invitation, but only a matter of your disposition.

You are safe to stand on the part of good fighting evil or on the part of evil opposing good but do not stand in between, you will be receiving all the blow.

The good should not be masquerading as evil for this is below their dignity and a sign of timidity nor should the evil cosmetize themselves as good as this is a sign of shame.

If what you are is shameful to behold, then consider a change and stop at nothing ensuring it is changed.

Nature has much respect for man and makes everything that is to the benefit of man to have upper hand to their opposition. Water is not stronger than fire but simply a matter of which man is more in need of at the time. **But for the law of nature, it would have been easier for fire to burn water than for water to quench fire.**

Darkness shows obeisance to light simply on grounds of human sight, and because it cannot afford to fight back, and more that he who refuses to see should not blame nature for inconsistency.

Light is the most potent plague of darkness, and renders all its opposition an effort in futility. You do not struggle with darkness, simply shine the light.

You might never realize the evils that have been perpetrated in the dark, until you bring in the light.

> *And be careful, for when darkness came upon the earth at the beginning, it rendered the earth formless and void until there was light.*

If you are of the substance of the earth, what plagues the earth can plague you! There are demons walking about whose only mission is to wreak havoc and cause evil. They are a part of your spiritual environment, never be ignorant of their activities.

86

PAINS

Humanity has had the peace it deserves though humans must continue to fight for the peace they want.

Every single man has a considerable amount, but as the tongue always traces the aching tooth,

> *the human mind is always directed to the areas that peace does not abound in the world of a man.*

Business is life and a relaxed mind should better have been death.

There is no state of absolute bedlam even in inanimate things and so the entropy of human life is only a proportion.

> *In any state of chaos you may find yourself, there is always a direction that is peaceful to the feel.*

There is a principle of super imposition of chaos, pain or conflict, that when the greater comes, the lesser that was once greater gets lost in the shadow of the latter.

Will the pains in your body stop you from fleeing to safety if you heard the firing of guns? In a moment the pains disappear and the body reunites for its good. **With a proper push, there is nothing a man cannot do or achieve.**

This is the consolation that accompanies every human pandemonium and part of it is always a reconsideration of factors and acceptance of your existence.

In whatever way you arrange for your peace, you find war and sorrow at the corners of your life.

The wars you see are the natural hostility of the world towards you, of which it is expected you can cope as nobody is naturally given more than he can carry.

As long as you continue to exist within the confines of the atmosphere, you will always find yourself harassed by powerful forces: the market forces, the spiritual forces, almost any force has its weight mounted on men in a way.

But if you could see what maggots do to the dead toad, you will never wish to die. People who dodged the stages of their development as well as those who had accepted positions higher than what they can attain will have difficulties with this, but there is no problem without a solution.

The solution is simply accepting your real self and disposing of the borrowed rope.

> *The pains you avoided were necessary to make you a true soldier in the necessary wars of life*

and thus you may find yourself grossly inadequate for the situation you are finding yourself.

There is a solution even to this. The war will not destroy you completely, but only reduce you to where you suited except you resist and hold on to your claim. In all these adversities, patience is the only necessary tool for you.

Be patient with yourself as well as patient with others.

You will not be happy realizing you hurt the wrong person and so must be a little patient to discover your real enemy, it possibly can be yourself.

Do not try to cheat on nature for

> *if nature had allowed itself to be cheated, some more trickish pallies would have taken everything even before you were born.*

There is a price for everything in life. You pay for the things you do, the things you fail to do, the things you buy, and the things you fail or choose not to buy.

Even pain can be pleasurable if it superimposes a nagging problem or situation.

Life is smarter than any man, this is why when men kill, maim and steal just to heap riches for their children, those things become useless even before they come of age, and they make a waste of them all the same.

87

PERFECTION

No man is perfect even when any man can be perfect. This is the difference between the ideal man and the practical man.

> *A building is as imperfect as where the imperfections started,*

where the builder treated important things as unimportant. Some buildings are imperfect right from the foundation except the plan which is ideal.

You may argue the ideal nature of plans as the architects are prone to making mistakes, but the mistakes spice the plan and a combination of them is the ideal.

> *But the first assignment for the man who seeks perfection, is to acquire good knowledge.*

Search and research again and again until there is nothing else to search for.

You can only do better when you know better and when you see the invisible, you will do the impossible.

> *Whatever you look-up to is the best until you are able to behold a better one.*

But you must be careful, for if there is always something better to change to, there will never be anything good enough to fight for.

A better line of adventure is along the string of conquest.

The plan of man is Ideal, drawn by the very best of all architects who spreads them as fitting pegs in fitting holes.

The real problem now exists in the understanding of the plan of nature and building to specification.

When you emulate that which flies, you will be able to fly no matter what. And if you emulate that which swims, you are bound to conquer the ocean. This is where premeditated acts constitute a virtue for the patient actor.

Because man does not really understand the plan of nature, we tend to skip those undertakings that would have best suited our plans, venturing into the easy way and taking everything for granted.

Imperfection is the wildest enemy of man, set by man, against himself.

The struggle to perfection is the narrowing of the gap between what you are and what you realize you should have been.

Though dignity is one, standards make the difference.

The vision of different men do not focus at the same lengths, and so, when you are struggling to what you have seen, do not compare yourself so much to other persons.

By coincidence you may see the same thing, but you may not see it in the same way. Some do not care so much as you do, we all do not have the same dreams.

When you have struggled to where some other person had been, do not stop where he stopped, for even when he was there, he saw greater heights he could not attain.

A step to overcome your imperfect nature leads to the attainment of standards.

Water goes downhill where it hopes to meet a river, and the easy way is a perfect way for any given fool.

The path of least resistance makes no adventure, for millions of miles water travels but makes no journey.

88

ADAPTATION

Where there is a son of wisdom, there is wisdom probably found.

Nothing really enters a place that is not for it, though we can prevent things from entering their place.

> *There is no better way to affect lives of others than in the choice of that which is your occupation.*

If you become a thief, a lot of people are going to lose their valuables to a wasteful spender.

A man's choice of occupation reflects to a large extent the spiritual occupants of his physical body.

These two may seem vain talk for things change in their status. Good can take up evil disposition as well as evil wearing the robe of grace.

The nature of things is unique, the past is important but the present determines what flows into the scene if only you never locked the doors against them in the past.

> *Some things in life need invitation to come, some more others seek invitation to come, but the bulk take the chances that there may be.*

You may lock the door against many but some are swift enough to fly in through the window.

The good patronize the good places that fit their nature, and thus the evil. It constitutes futility, dragging good to evil or evil to good unless you can change their position.

> *You will never understand putrefaction until you see it as a form of adaptation; if I won't go away, then it has to be my way or my life on the line.*

You have much to learn from microbes, they often survive because they do not just enter a place and go to sleep; they fight their way until they gain control.

If the world does not fight corruption the same way she fought putrefaction, no anti-corruption campaign will ever succeed.

But if we let the system collapse, we all have got something to lose. You cannot cure real sickness with palliatives.

When the bad enters a good place, it either changes to suit it or should better leave for its safety.

It is only in the gathering of simple good ones that evil can dread, but the strength that is expected of the good is what humanity lacks the most.

An evil man is as good as a rabble rouser and a schemer, while the good is like a patient dog, but how do we fit patience into a world of rush.

James, I pity those who spend hours in the shrines praying for prosperity and seeking peace. This is one reason deceivers will continue to proliferate with the empty promises of instant wealth.

> *It is not the wealth of this life that hates man, it is man that has deprived himself of wealth.*

Nobody gives wealth, not even the spirits, for wealth is a spirit in itself. Simply change the orientation of your life to suit peace and prosperity, you find them coming to dine and stay.

> *If you need money, then sell what you have, and if you have nothing to sell, then create one.*

A common man will trek miles upon miles daily to fetch from a running spring but the wise will dig to the spring right at his backyard.

*Do not accept what you never worked for, it will only come
to scatter that which it never gathered.*

You can be anything you want to be in this life, if only you use the
time you have well.

You have got enough time for something, but not for everything.

89

LOVE IV

When it has to do with love affair, I take extra time to fashion out that which suits the desires of men.

The love that we owe each other is in stages and we build those stages by our gestures.

> *I hardly find love in the marriages of rich men except those who had once suffered the scourges of poverty in peace and harmony.*

No man is too rich to be poor nor is any man too poor to be rich. Either in riches or poverty, love is unique but desires take different forms with lust as its principal.

Sometimes I advise any man to be rich, for in this, even a woman who hates you the most will pretend and stay just to have a fair share of the riches if only she does not kill you to take it all.

Love is the soothing, the healing, the care, the affection, those little kindnesses and the tenderness. This is where I see the poor search for love and the rich lust after many and is never satisfied.

> *There is this bitter thing about being rich, when you realize you can't have everything.*

One evil I hate so much is the men who push out the women who bore with them during the drought as soon as the fields start to yield. If nature will agree to change its laws, I will suggest it should punish these ones with death, though he does not spare them abject poverty in the long run.

When love advances to a stage of absorption, self-denial and holistic unification, hardly can any force push them apart. First sight is no love but the expression of the efficiency of your natural power to desire, while the first impression that we count is a drama of intoxication.

Your outward appearance is what attracts, but your inward beauty is what will keep your catch.

A picture can do many magic, but it should not be too different from reality.

'One' is love and nothing outside this.

To see with one eye, hear with one ear, smell with one nose, feel with one skin and reason with one mind is

unity in diversity and a combination of colors in white light, the secret of true love.

If you happen to live with a woman who is exactly like you, then you will certainly lose the beauty of life.

It does not matter what people think, it feels good to be loved by someone. Love is indeed the medicine of life!

If you are sophisticated enough as I pray you will be, you would not read love from an open teeth. Even snakes and vampires open their teeth when they want a bite, the fact that she smiles at you does not mean she is in love.

I give you the secret meaning to the true word, love is a command, not a feeling!

<u>**love is a learned act not an emotional state.**</u>

Hold this key and life will be sweet. The idea of falling is human fantasy that holds no water.

Falling in today and falling out tomorrow, without commitment from the heart, you won't find them together the next summer.

A man that falls in love is likely making a mistake he will choose to live with or live in regrets.

The Holy book commands you to love, it is the will of God for you. You can befriend fantasy, but be sure you marry reality.

Do not accept the love of a woman that does not complete your other half. But if she does complete, whatever she says is what you could not say, and what she sees is what you could not see. Her reasoning is the other part of your reasoning that is needed to make a full sense and the very best.

She does not complement you if she cannot contradict you, for you will never see your error if love does not point to you the other way. If she is too careful to make mistake, there are too many things she is trying to hide.

Love is not for perfect beings, else God could have profess his to angels and not men.

He who divides the soul is a murderer that lives to be feared.

Whatever love affair splits without pain was probably a disguised parasitic game.

Compatibility is the ability to manage differences and not the harmony of character, and the ability to understand that is a test of your maturity.

Conscience is an open wound that only truth can heal, delay will make it stink.

90

CHOICE IV

He makes a good choice that chooses the very best in the market even at the cost of all he has gotten.

It is indecent to feel pity for the things that appear substandard to your yardstick, for they probably make the best for the next man.

The best you choose might not be the very best but

the best of the leftovers make the best for the next chooser.

Where lies the pleasure in choosing what you do not love?

Do not let people deceive you into coping and do not deceive yourself for there is nothing to cope with in a love affair. Whatever is in your possession demands your care and attention as an end not a means to an end of a fool.

If what you have at hand is not what pleases your soul, you are already at war with yourself.

Where will you get the strength to force yourself? Grow up and live up to your standards, understanding the power of choice and the happiness it brings.

Do not let people dump on you and do not dump on yourself. Respect the choices of your body members and understand that they get sick each time you dump just about anything on them, and so will you if you dump just about anything on yourself. **Many people will get mad at you when**

you do not let them dump their shit on you, but that is their disease, let them take the pills.

You can afford to please every other person, but do not displease yourself by so doing.

You live with the consequence of your choice be it good or evil while others take their share and are gone.

It is a mark of unwittiness to make your choice for the sake of the satisfaction of others while jeopardizing your own peace and tranquility. There are times for sacrifices, but the proper sacrifices will always leave you better.

We accept who puts a woman to the family way should marry her. However this may apply, it is a gross sign of indiscipline of your members if you should carelessly go into a woman who is more or less a nightmare, as you may choose to call her after the consequence of your stupidity has come to lime light.

It is embarrassing to die in the hand of an amateur. But if you must play the game, then play it well even with the very best player that there may be.

There is nothing cheap about cheap articles, they always take more from you later for little or no satisfaction.

If you want to eat a frog, then go for the fattest ones.

If you go ahead to choose below your choice, whatever you may be doing to derive pleasure from it may prove abortive because your soul is somewhere searching for what it wants in other to please itself.

This has been the bane of many marriages but it must not be yours.

Do not ever conclude your life because of your present situation.

Things will always change for the better if you have enough faith.

But I will advise any man towing the path of faith to first have a keen vision, do all in your power to see what you believe in physical or spiritual, for what you cannot see you may never get no matter how strongly you convince yourself.

There is always something sweet about that which is eaten in the secret, and this is the confusion of the unfaithful. Be careful.

If you must choose,

choose the best but never between all that is yours.

Develop the habit of looking for something in life and not everything. And when you have seen that one important thing, take it with gratitude and go your way.

Life is too short for any man to experience all things.

Do not form the habit of making an all-in-one choice; in these ones, the important features might never work.

91

PROFIT

Seek the maximum profit that there is in whatever course you undertake. There are natural laws of cause and effect, or deeds and consequence to be precise.

> *There should be no food for lazy man, but rich men capitalize on the labor of poor ones.*

A good profit is a product of good bargain, and when you come to an end make sure you pay what was agreed.

Every man deserves the fruit of his labor but must not deprive the other of his possession.

Evil men should be paid of their evil but who pays back the evil is evil in himself that must be paid back.

It is because men started to stack wealth to themselves that thieves emerged and from thieves proceeded hostility and insecurity.

There is enough in the world for everyone, the problem is that some people pack to themselves in a day, what they can never spend in their whole life time.

> *Pleasure is the father of materialism, from which is all forms of corruption, a product of the raw instinct of lower beings.*

Some deeds are better not done even when they give the promise of profiting course.

We accept the end justifies the means, but we hardly meet the end in human affairs.

The ultimate end is death but death itself is not the end of life. Life continues after death and

some profits drag mounts of losses along with them.

There is no gain without pain and the risk of investment is the joy of interest.

It is human virtue to decipher real gain from gainful loss whichever comes the first; to loose in gain and gain in loss.

Do not accept a profit that does not profit you.

You must learn early in life to say no to an evil gain, this is one personal wisdom that will bring you enduring riches. Ignorance is no excuse and labor is the price of wage.

Wage without labor is the lure of slavery and the easiest way to deceive a man and take even the much he has from him.

Do not accept an offer without asking what the other will take from you and even when he says nothing, look at him the second time.

Favors are not meant to be returned, but every man expects to reap someday from where he had sowed.

It would be better not to be receiving gifts for it makes us debtors like it or not, and debtors cannot stand on their ground.

Gifts have blinded the wise and bought the justice of the just.

But for the sake of humanity, we are obliged to receive gifts, but return as soon as possible to claim back your ground.

Just a small story of a vulture on top a palm tree: It was seriously beaten by the rain and swore by the gods of the land that as soon as the rain stops, it was going to build itself a house. But as soon as the rain stopped and the sun begins to shine, its wings dried and it flew away in search of the next carcass to devour, forgetting it will rain again.

Can you stick to your course in spite of the storm? Or can you sustain the decisions you made in tough times when the good times return?

Don't be just another vulture except you want to grow feathers and long nails and a bald head.

Tough times always visit men, people or nations who don't make tough decision and stick to them.

92

WISDOM III

Try as much as you can to walk with the wise for that is how you will be the wise yourself.

I am a man in my world, and my success in life is not tide to any man or system of the world, but God alone.

Good ends are made in participation in a good course while

the company of evil transfers evil instincts.

As iron sharpens iron, so does a friend bless the countenance of his friend.

Knowledge is an infection, the symptoms may tarry if you fight back, but some of it will certainly show when the environment is conducive.

The things we learn are the things we do, but those who refuse to learn are taught by ease.

Watch what you watch especially when it is not what you want.

Your eye is the window of the mind. And when you open it to thieves, you are bound to come to losses; and when the mind has been stolen, the body will follow to destruction.

Ease can never teach what is good but gives you what it takes to make you his slave.

Knowledge is a well that any man can scoop but ignorance is a pressure against human affairs.

Those who fix their eyes on the light are enlightened but darkness will not find it a pleasure letting its captives free.

There is vision in darkness but hardly away from where you are standing.

The dark can swear to contention but light is a sweet sensation.

It is virtuous to leave dark into light but not without your effort and co-operation.

Light and darkness do not struggle, they have their standards.

Darkness itself cannot stand the presence of light and takes to flight as soon as it appears.

To overcome his weakness, darkness has taken to the study of persuasion and empty promises, the practice of deception. There is a point you get to in the world of darkness, and it will be difficult to appreciate the goodness of light anymore; watch your steps.

James, those who stay in darkness can tell stories of non-existent virtuality.

Those who see the light are not the best brains but he who can move from darkness to light. It will be human kindness to lead those in the dark to light, but how do you convince them that there is a better place uphill with a cooler sensation?

Even after conviction, you need his effort to get him up the hill and not without his co-operation.

Many people leave the light to darkness in pursuance of empty promises. Light has taken so much from darkness and so darkness has now come to the knowledge of how to steal from light; many people actively and openly recruit for the devil these days.

A little away from the light is now enough for darkness to take hold of you.

Do not take league with evil, do not even attempt to sign a contract of a few days, for you will end up buried in it your whole life.

Resist with your whole power the pleasures of sin, nobody has ever benefited from such at the end.

93

KNOWLEDGE IV

He who hides his knowledge should better have been stupid for this would have afforded him a better state of comfort.

> *The solution to human problems is the knowledge that exists in human minds.*

It is all about what we know but what you know cannot pay the price.

> *No man should boast of having beyond what he has given for the rest might be mere illusions. If you cannot show what you have, then you have nothing to show.*

A milk can cannot represent a tin of milk yet until it is open and the content confirmed to be milk.

It is funny how nature keeps its things in the hiding and might possibly be because it does not want human minds to be lazy. **You cannot solve a puzzle with missing pieces; when you follow a matter, know the whole story. When you need to know what you do not know, then ask from who knows and be patient until you are told.**

Discovery is human business and the more we get is the more we want.

The trend of discovery is like climbing a giant tree, we can tell how we started to climb but no man has gotten to the leaves. At one point of discovery, there is a presentation of several branches and in all these, you can only climb a branch at a time. This is one reason you need companions who will take to other branches but you may soon lose sight of your friends due to further branching.

Anything zealed has no usefulness to man.

Try as much as you can to avoid a kind of learning that does not present practical solutions, but follow the light and come out of the darkness of your mind that you may present to the world what you have gotten.

Only when fountains are opened can we drink of its waters.

There are fountains of knowledge and wisdom everywhere but what you can open is what you have gotten.

A good understanding of your undertaking will make you outstanding in the outcome.

The deeper you go into a matter the brighter you will shine soaring in the skies. Great heights must first explore great depths.

A man's ignorance is his limitation, his unbelief is his weakness. If a man can know all things, then he can do all things.

The omnipotence of God is inherent in his Omniscience.

You cannot know much about God without knowing about yourself.

The godly character of man begins to play out when abundant of right knowledge is found in him.

Nobody prays to a god who knows not how to do a thing. Nobody begs from who obviously has nothing to give.

The man who gives a map to a pilgrim is a good man.

The most important part of the map is the **point**, without which it is useless all the same.

If he who has the light will not let it shine, then darkness will continue to roam human minds.

Lighting another man's candle does not make yours to glow dimmer. If you cannot wait to light another's candle because of the storm, soon you will have no one to light yours.

Unless you are ready to burn yourself away, just like the candle in your hand, you may never be able to light the way for others.

If we mine ourselves the way we mine the earth, we will discover within better treasures in store.

TEMPTATION

94

What constitutes human temptation is an expression of the state of indiscipline.

Knowledge of what is good is the virtue that every man should seek, but the knowledge of evil too will be beneficial to him.

Since knowledge is an ambivalent phenomenon, the choice of dexterity to levity is what the discipline of members can guarantee.

Anything is no choice and not all choices can make the business of living.

We know what is good as well as that which is bad. We know those things we should get and those we should not get even when they are within the bounds of our strength.

> *In order to overcome temptation, you will have to draw a*
> *line of standard.*

You have to be able to tell yourself the difference between what is yours and that which is not yours, and you must start from handling your own business properly.

> *Beware of your powers, it is the same that bring sudden*
> *destructions upon a man when misused.*

When you turn a stone into bread at the devil's command, it can be sweet in your mouth, but a bitter poison in your stomach, your meal of death.

Be careful of the things you do, even when it is within your power to do same.

Multiple standards is a man's tachity, but the poorest choice for a strong character.

Emptiness has no place in human life as failure to get what you should get will automatically fill the gap with what you should not get.

A man's mind is either full of sense or nonsense but a mixture of these is the perfect state of nature.

To expel nonsense, you will have to apply sense with a greater force.

There are many vices we attribute to temptation and we employ the devil to overcome our weakness. The only strength of the devil is his advantage of the weaknesses of men. The devil would not be seen to be strong if men were not as weak as they have made themselves.

I find it funny terming theft and sexual immorality a temptation when indeed they constitute disgraces.

Without discipline, it is very hard for any man to attain destiny.

There might just be enough gas to take you from where you are to where you ought to be. But if you spend it on pleasure rides, you might get stuck where there is no station to refill.

We know the time to sow and are sure of food in the harvest if we nourish the crops.

He who does not have a thing should work and be patient enough until he can get it and what we force on ourselves will find a way of leaving us even if it will take it to destroy us in order to have its freedom.

Wise men steal from nature while foolish ones steal from humans.

But even when you steal from nature, it should be out of perfect timing and to your advantage, and be sure to return to it as soon as possible or it will take from you in a way that is possible.

The greatest wisdom to apply in acquisition is that there is no grant of ownership of material things to any mortal man.

All you can ever have is meant for temporal use and then you leave them behind for only God knows who.

If you steal too much of the night, you might end up sleeping the permanent sleep of death.

Give to Caesar that which belongs to Caesar, and to God, that which belongs to God.

When you assume an evil disposition, do not count it a surprise finding yourself in the scene of evil and in fact, one of the actors.

Do not tempt the devil, for it has never been written anywhere that he ever overcome temptation.

One of the hardest stunts in life is to try to trick the devil; he is the master in the art, you might be working against your very self.

Truth is the greatest weapon against evil, especially when you tell it in raw terms.

95

FOUNDATION

The beginning of a man's life is important as well as the end. The foundation of a house is as important as the roof. Castles are not built in the air nor are roofs put on trees. I am a builder and God is a master builder. I have seen my works suffer cracks under weather so I am not surprise when I see cracks in men who walk under the sun.

A man that wants his shoot to grow must learn to water its roots. Without horizontal peace, there is no vertical uprising.

> *You must make peace with God, your source, whatever you conceive him to be! It is the roots that supply and sustain the tree.*

Your foundation starts from where you realize yourself.

The very day you comprehend who you are, is when you should look forward to what you would like to be.

You must consider the weight of your building and consider what it is going to stand upon, you must be sure the foundation would endure considering the storms of life that will surely come, of which if they shift away, you are bound to crash.

Nature has not pitched the foundation of any man on a ground too porous to build upon.

> *The only reason humans do not survive, is that they build the wrong house on top of the right foundation or the right house on top of the wrong foundation.*

Before you take unto what you would like to be, first consider what you are and the strength that there is at your disposal to get there.

Do not put faith in any thing called man and let all favors that come to you be accidentals of your disposition.

Wisdom is knowing your problems and seeking out the proper ways of solving them.

A man's number one problem in life is lack of knowledge!

If a man can know all things then he can have all things.

It is a shameful thing to ask for favor in life but if by your disposition it comes to you, be happy to receive it but do not expect any other in the future.

Life is all improvement, development and stages attainment.

Do not joke with your naturally endowed talents. It might be the only currency you have to buy the good things of life. But if you polish your diamond, you can buy yourself a castle.

Stick to your talent and the source and you can securely walk through life.

Many people have often told you to stand on the shoulders of great and successful men, a sure way to succeed; but you must first find out if they would let you stand on their shoulders, for many who do, often end up under their feet. It is in fact better to stand on the shoulders of those who have gone beyond, for they, even if they do not like your face, can hardly do anything about it.

I do not like a kind of man that everything should workout fine for him. In a man's life, some things have to go the wrong way in order that he may learn.

Bitter experiences stick to the human memory but sweet sensations are mere trifles.

Caution is indeed the watchword, if you must get to the other side of life. Each stage you find yourself in life is a preparation for the next stage.

Do not walk away from a scene without a lesson to learn, things do not happen for nothing in life.

If you find joy, take it as much as you can, for after it will come pain.

And if by luck you find pain your way, accept it as much as you can for only after this will you find joy in full.

> *For as long as the earth endures and the sun rises in the east across the sky, seed time and harvest, summer and winter, day and night, joy and sadness will never cease to visit the life of a man.*

You can only trace the starting point of your life but you cannot tell the end. Even if you should have somebody to tell you how and where your life will end, you find it hard to believe; but if you believe, you may end your life before the end.

You can tell the plans you have for tomorrow, but you cannot tell what plans tomorrow has for you.

Search for the gold in that mud you find yourself and the stars in the scar of your life.

Do not be afraid of the scars that the battles of life can bring to you, champions are born of the heat of challenges; there are no victories without battles and no heroes whose songs where never born of uncommon victories. The world is an arena, a grand theater for any man to proof his marksmanship.

If you are not satisfied with where you are in life, then transplant yourself; this is allowed physically and spiritually by the gift of will.

> *Until you take time to polish the very diamond in your life, you will never realize the glitters that in it abound.*

96

HOPE

One thing about you is that you ask so many questions at a time, but even this is not a wrong thing to do.

Only in questions do we find answers and in answers, find questions. Even questions are far better than complaints for complaint are useless dissipation of your useful energy. An average life on earth is a question begging for answers, and finding answers to life questions is a great business.

> *Follow the process of life diligently, for this is the sure way; ask any great man standing, and he will tell you he did the same.*

You asked if I should wake up one day to behold my only hope, my source of refuge and my only comfort has been terminated, what I would do?

James, hope is like a tree, it never ends except at the branches. Hope is that silver cord upon which is suspended the lives of men.

One hope takes a man to a place that he may find the beauty that exists in other hopes. It is always frustrating when you stand there trying to find an answer to that pressing problem, but if only you go further, you will know better, if you look further, you will see better.

This is the kind of thing I would like to do;

> *If I should find that my hope of living is gone, I will have the hope of dying instead of killing myself.*

If my refuge should be gone, then it was not the better thing that should have come to me and it is better that it is gone that my refuge may find me. If my only comfort should be gone, I will be the happiest man for having an opportunity of experiencing the discomforts of life.

The important thing is not the discomforts that come your way, but how you respond to them your own way. Wise people do not avoid these things, but they confront them.

Great minds do not complain about these things, but only change them into questions and seek their answers. The search for answers is the surest highway of great opportunities in life.

You should only overcome your weaknesses but should not avoid them.

As long as you are alive, nothing really is gone, but some will be useless to hold back when they have concluded their part.

When things leave their places, allow them to go their way. Struggling to hold them back will be a vain drag yet until they meet the wrong side of their infatuation.

Marrying a prostitute is sweet from the way they respond to your needs, you only know your mistake when you really want a settle home, for then she will be gone.

Hope often disappoints because we hope the wrong way, spelling out the end of a matter that is beyond our control and at the same time doing nothing to interfere in the course to suit our purpose.

Next time you hope, be sure someone has done the work that will bring about the manifestation of your dream. Hope not worked for is tantamount to frustration.

There is a natural order in the universe, from which is distilled the basic principles of life and living. They are eternal laws because they have never changed to suit any man's wimps and caprices.

No matter how many times you stumble upon a rolling stone, it will still roll on at the slightest chance.

Rolling might possibly be their nature. And if you refuse them the manifestation of their character, be ready to pay with your life for the delays you have caused them. Do not play the fool ignoring obvious signs; do not live in denial, there is no mercy for fools.

> *It is in the character of snakes to bite, and of scorpions to stink; so be careful the next time you stumble upon one; they are the same, both the spiritual and the physical, you must identify them on time!*

Some are just like the mouse; they blow you physically as if to soothe, but they are the same people biting you spiritually, the cause of your pains.

97

PLANNING

He who does not plan, is planning to fail but he who plans to succeed is failing from the start.

Plans are useless, but planning is everything. There are no perfect plans in life, only it is always better to keep planning all the way. One wisdom in planning is to know the bigger plan and plant your plan. If you know where the wind is going in life, then you will sail through life without stress.

Things are never the way they appear as the critical parts of things often take to cryptophilial stands. If your plan is sponsored by an ambition, then do not be the gatherer, be the hunter, provide for the interest of ambitions. Since everybody these days is only interested in success at whatever cost, then the best commodity to trade upon is the elixir of success. This should give you a vision.

Who you are is important with respect to what you want. Wants, is the portion of every man but many often want out of proportion.

> *The variation of want and resource brings the option of choice and choices are complements of plans. Small pictures are useless without the bigger picture in sight, and a goal to pursue. Always be sure you get something for something and nothing for nothing.*
>
> *Success is the portion of every man but those who cannot pay the price.*

In other to efficiently actualize your strategies, first understand your dignity.

Evil does not work for Kings nor do virtues work for demons.

Try as much as you can to plan in accordance with what you are.

Wishes are no horses nor beggars better choosers. Do not be too big to beg when it becomes necessary, do not expect pardon from enemies, only buy yourself sometime for your next move or backup.

Many things that work for the other persons may never work for you simply because you are not who they are.

Men are not what they seem, and it is very difficult to spot a true child in the midst of children; look before you leap.

When you are dealing with the victims of life, you may realize uncertainties abound with men.

If a man is too careful to lose, play along, he will soon lose to you.

The clothes that suit you may not suit the others and borrowed robes are what they are nor matter how you turn them.

Even when you claim you have put things in their place, learn to fix your mind on success and failures.

Things are as right as they appear to you but not often right in themselves.

Strategies are the words we give to thoughts but things work
in a different way.

You must understand that the world is an ever-changing medium, far different from the chemicals in your laboratories. Market systems are ever-changing, technologies are ever-changing, the producers are ever reducing their quantities and sellers increasing price, the environment is ever-changing, and none of it will be tomorrow the way it is today. Human reactions are not chemical reaction, don't be too sure!

Every other person is planning one thing or the other, and they all affect your plan. Men are afraid of many things, get them to relax and take your share.

There are two markets that will never collapse in the world, fears and wants. People will always be afraid and in want.

When your plan depends on a failing system, you have already failed all the same except that is your opportunity.

It is better to start, fail, learn and try again, than to plan for a lifetime.

In whatever you want to do, understand that you are an imperfect being working on imperfect speculations.

Things either work or they do not work but never a do or die affair.

Sometimes you have to fail in one course so that you can succeed in another if you are quick in understanding.

I have heard the story of a man who sold his farmland for a few hundred dollars because it was not yielding him much and moved to another place. The man who bought that farm dug a deeper well and discovered huge deposit of crude oil.

Sometimes when you appear superficially unproductive and unattractive, there might be huge treasures within begging for attention.

The solution to most life problems lies deep within the problem and you can succeed if only you will dig deeper.

In life it is good to know your content; this is often not unconnected with your problems.

98

MENTALITY

The things that make the mind busy are the ones apart from its reaching.

People seldom content with the things they have at hand even when a bird at hand, it is said, is worth the two in the bush. Even this should not serve as a discouragement for the ability to get the other two; these will make you the happier.

Desires do not constitute vices but the actualization of that beyond your power.

> *The human mind indeed is a bundle of desires, and desire, the driving force of human actions. A man without motivation will live and die in obscurity despite the vastness of his potentials.*

It is self-actualization to look for things at a distance but be careful to walk in order to reach them.

If you move at things beyond your steps, you may pass-by them before you know.

> *The targets of the mind are corked unbranded cans; you may hardly sense the smell or know the substance in them except that which you suppose.*

Many beautiful things are not beautiful in themselves nor the ugly ones as ugly as they appear.

Avoid prejudice with all the power in you; do not conclude that which you have not examined.

There could be functional similarities, he could have the manners, but it does not mean he is a monk.

Watch, but do not judge. This is why you need to eat of the porridge before you can really say its taste is the like.

Even when you taste of the pudding do not expect a universal sensation for even when it means the meat to you, it can be poison to somebody somewhere.

Do not judge a man by your own standards; if he is too short for you, you could also be too tall for him, and none of these is good enough.

This is even the more reason you should not be busy about clothes that do not suit you. Some clothes were strictly made so that they do not suit you but should suit some other person somewhere. Keeping these ones may be useless to you for they only consume the space of some fitting ones.

Some human desires are hard, some dry and many vain but yet they all constitute your desires.

It is not enough to avert uncertainty for even certainties may never work for many minds.

> *Security is a practical deception, one button that drives men into making difficult decisions.*

Do not be angry with your mind for what it desires nor your eyes for what it sees, it is their dignity to see and desire even the things that are losses and gains.

In gains are losses and in losses, gain, from whichever angle you may love to see it. To the man who has much is much to lose, and so are his sorrows and woes.

To one it is half full and to another it is half empty, just a function of perspectives.

> *You never see what you never looked for even when it is right there in front of you, and at times you may not even see what you are looking for because it is not what you wanted to see.*

The next time you have a picture in your mind, ask your mind how it came about that picture, that may be where your deception started.

Thoughts have generated dreams that have apprehended men their whole life.

If you should know where your dreams come from, then you will be very careful the way you interpret them.

Let not your life follow the interpretation of dreams, you are most likely to end in frustration this way. So many people access your spirit man in dreams, you might never know who exactly is talking to you and why?

99

LIFE

There are not more precious things than the ability of living though many love to play the game of Russian roulette. Soldiers come, soldiers go, but the armies still remain.

You may choose to die and go, but do not expect the world to die with you.

It is a foolish thing men talk so much about the end of the world, and forget that it is even men that end every single day, a better thing to ponder upon; this world who knows it?

Don't be a party to them who only talk about the woes of life, there is good abounding in the world, follow after these.

Circumstances come to meet life and circumstances will leave life behind.

It is beautiful that things should be everywhere, and important too that you never get some of them in order that others may get them. Things come to life to make it and others have to leave life in other that life may be better.

Whichever comes and whichever goes, it is your position to take advantage of all.

There are no more advantages in the things that you cannot get than there is in things you have gotten at hand. But whichever comes first is for the sake that you may use them to climb to the other or develop them to be better than others.

Living is not a circumstance nor is it a chance to be alive.

Life is made and it is real so that in it you take the chances to immortalize your mortal nature.

The only world a man has is his life breath.

The only chance he has gotten to set fire on the world and prove to many generations that he existed. It determines what the gains and the losses he may accomplish.

Those who stern to life may never have anything to live upon and those who are careless with life may never live to regret their stand.

Life is the means to all ends, and an end made is an accomplished life. The best way to live is to live running after something, just one important thing that will make you happy.

The most important thing is not your living but what you make out of it. But you have to be living before you can make anything out of life.

But whatever you do in life, deliver the message, accomplish the mission!

Death men do not tell tales.

It is the living that become legends, and the stars are the ones that stick to the sky no matter what.

Take it easy, life is not in a hurry.

It is slow and steady that wins in the long race of life.

Win the little battles as they come, someday you will win the war. Avoid battles that are not a part of your campaign, you can never fight everything. Enjoy every opportunity that comes your way, and when you come to the bridge, cross it; it is part of the life bargain.

When you have found the way, let nothing stop you!

100

DISCIPLINE II

Many great minds led their lives better in descent poverty than indecent riches.

> *Everything is possible for a man to get, but not all that a man has is honorable to him*.

I have seen a lot of this kind of men whose riches are the greatest dishonor of their lifetime.

Decency is a necessary part of the life of a man who wishes to preserve his dignity and uphold his integrity in whatever course he undertakes.

> *To be a prince does not consist in being the son of a King.*

We give same to these, simply because we feel there is no alternative to it, but there is more than this in a princely life.

A true prince is one who has the training to take a kingdom and hold it together. Lost are those times when kings trained their princes on what it takes to be king, but now what we have are kings who do not understand one alphabet in the word. How then can they give what they don't have? We have generals and presidents whose children only know how to sniff drugs and get drunk, what a decadent world!

There are many kingdoms in life without kings, if you find one vacant throne, then do not hesitate to crown yourself the king. There is a kingdom for every man in purpose on earth.

It is decent to lead a higher degree virtuous life, but it is original to feel the weight of corruption.

It is not enough to resign to solitary confinement but a normal man must live in the world of humans.

Discipline is a sure highway that leads to destiny; as no man, whatever gods be his sponsor, can attain his God given destiny without discipline.

But know that although discipline will lead you on the path to destiny, discipline is no destiny!

A man's gifts are not his calling, but a man is given many talents to help him to live out his calling. No man can estrange his talents from his calling.

Leading a saintly life does not consist in avoiding sinful occasions but in confronting sinful habits and getting them to succumb to your standings.

James, If I were a nun, I would not choose to live in the nunnery, but I would see how I can live in a brothel without going into the ways of the scarlet woman. If everyone was hiding away, who then will make the world system work?

It is not enough to have everything you need at your disposal, but I would be the happier if I can stay in poverty without going into alms begging.

When you are always protected from yourself, you will live and die without knowing your worth. You can never tell a good dog till you leave it with a bag of bones.

A saint should know how to steal and if possible, should steal a holy life.

A judge should know how to be a criminal so as to know who he is dealing with, when he is judging crimes.

Those who have never married should never fix the rules of marriage nor those who have never loved tell the pains of passion.

Hard men are never those who have never tasted fire, but those who in doing thus, have been able to come out unburnt and unbroken.

101

LAW

One thing I am yet to see, since the day I was born, is the state that has a rigid law.

The laws of nature are standing but there is always yards of attachment to provide for changes in circumstance. A man's behavior is a function of what surrounds him. It is the folly of many to believe they can never change; for worse or for better.

A particular law suits a particular time and

> *It is a sign of ignorance to hold unto old laws when it is obvious that circumstances have changed.*

But there are people who are resistant to change, preferring to dwell in their comfortable mess whatever the consequences may be.

Man indeed should be strong, making policies for himself and living up to them. He should seek to please every man the much he can but should spare nothing in displeasure to himself.

Right laws may hurt the wrong person and wrong laws may consequently, hurt the right person.

This does not mean there should be no laws for laws are made for order and order is necessary for every human.

> *Acting against your will is never a sign of weakness, nor holding stiff to your standard strength of character.*

Certain experiences trigger policies but this we should understand was based on our comprehension of the circumstance.

But any man that allows himself to be pushed around, changing his plans and policies with every appearing circumstance is heading the way of disaster; for the law itself should be the anchor of the society, preventing you from being push around by the wimps and caprices of other men.

What could be expected from a state where thieves make the laws that govern the crime, for looking around I see a thousand justices but no judge among men. A country is decaying whose judges are given to bribery and corruption, where is the hope of the common man?

Man makes the society as much as the society makes man.

There are spiritual laws for the spiritual and physical laws for the physical, all working perfectly within their realms and domains.

You can never make the best judgment out of your own laws but judgment is necessary for choice.

To judge a man rightly, first try to understand him and not what he has done nor what he appears to be.

It is better to judge circumstances than man and this is why the best of relationships are made when coming from clean slates.

To avoid regrets, be patient with your judgment less you hurt the wrong person. But if you can afford to be merciful, this is what you would expect, it is much better than justice.

You need a perfect knowledge in order to pass a righteous judgment in your integrity; there is no judge like God Almighty.

102

COMMITMENT

One evil I have seen in the world is that people do not keep their words. This is the worst of all indiscipline and people who indulge in it should consider themselves worse than the worst imbecile.

It is goodness to make a good selection of words when you are dealing with the minds of men.

Some people take pleasure in watching you go the other way while what they mean is this very direction.

Crafty men take pride in persuasion, use of ambivalent terms and equivocation.

You are bound to meet these kinds everyday especially in the law profession; not to worry, simply pay them with the same coin.

The techniques of swerve – and - swing are employed for the contacts of make - and - break. Do not go into love affair without a promise nor undertake a contract without a written agreement.

Many people just take to confusion right from the start and you wonder when they will be sure of what they want.

The things that are not there are not there no matter how much you try.

A good beginning makes a good ending.

A love affair is not like the court of law, and silence does not mean yes.

A man that refuses to say a thing is looking for an easy way out, but is even better than one who says what he does not mean.

> *If you agree to bear with a man while you are still blind in love, then make up your mind to bear with him when you are able to see who he is.*

Love is living for another, and lust is living on another; to be happy when he is happy and to be there when she is in need is the walk upon the highway of love.

> *When a man is satisfied, he will never ask for more.*
> *The burden of lust is how to keep your victim coming for more when he is already looking elsewhere for the next victim.*

If you are not the first, you might not be the last; a man searching for pleasure will never be satisfied with pleasure.

One thing you must keep in mind when contracting is that, the other person has not told you everything and the ones that he has not told you, are the ones you have to find out yourself.

It is better not to promise than to promise without fulfilling. We may term this to be swiftness ignoring the idiocy of our actions.

Promises done either whole heartedly or not are counting against you so long as the other person takes your words into account.

Agreements too are binding in as much as they were agreed upon and ignorance is no excuse.

Whenever you have doubts in an affair, try to relax your progress until the airs are cleared.

The promises you made and the agreement are the only source of strength and justification in weakness and tribulation.

You have come all this way, it is time to hear the truth that the only promise you should keep so dear to your heart is the one that you made to yourself, to love this imperfect person no matter what it may be. But if you didn't come this far, then you haven't gone far anyway.

Try as much as you can not to swim across the river if you have nothing in sight to hold unto should your strength fail you halfway.

Watch your confidence and be sure it can be trusted; you do not speed on the highway of life with a faulty break and expect a miracle to pop-up in the face of disaster.

103

TRUST

It is a mark of great art to comprehend the expressions on the human face.

The human mind is often busy in formulation and some signals find a way of escaping to the face even after intense suppression.

By suppression, I mean that not every thoughts of a man's heart can be found expressed on his face.

The beauty of this art is in the investigation not stories.

The things you see are not what they are if you care to realize. And,

Streams of emotion lurk behind mild smile.

Every man is a puzzle to solve, so you do not ignore even the piece of character you find here and there.

Might be if you can put the pieces together, you can have an idea of what you are dealing with.

It is hard to let loose of our emotions since human beings are so insincere.

The very moment you start to shed tears of true love is when they start to play on you.

Evil thoughts too can be seen on the face, but evil thoughts are often suppressed for fear of suspicion should they not be the real actors.

It is hard to trust in the world but you must trust in order to succeed, either in God or in man.

Since people are simply obsessed with the expressions they find on the face, prostitutes and assassins have taken to smiles. Unusual smiles are signs of evil, while unusual muteness are signs of depressions.

These in themselves are not what they have always been, but my own comprehension.

> *It is hard to know those we love since we have refused to love those we know.*

If you do not know a man too well, then do not dump yourself on him. Even if love is riding you on high gear, do not trade your weakness.

When a man is in love with an angel, let it be that way and don't come up with the story of a prostitute.

Knowledge is the root of corruption and is still corrupting the mind. Never give the right information to the wrong man.

And do not expect a mind that has been corrupted to continue to act the same, the least he can do is pretend, but not for long.

Those who decline your offers in the day spend hours thinking of you before the drag of sleep.

Every expression is important and tends to be saying something, but do not expect from it everything.

If you want to know everything, then ask questions, but they will only tell you what they feel you should hear. **Above all, I must give you this warning, you must never put your trust in anything and anyone that is capable of change. If it can change, someday it will change!**

104

DECEPTION

From the fullness of the heart, the mouth speaks and the mistakes made, are the ones that escaped undetected.

We often wonder why people say different things but I am certain too that I have never said anything I never heard or formulated sometime.

Many indeed are the thoughts of a man's heart and none dies either good or evil, but only waiting patiently for the right signal to explode.

I may talk of the right signal, but

> *when hell is full, even the wrong signal may be enough for it to let loose its content.*

There could be an establishment of what can be termed 'the unconscious consciousness' when it has to do with talks and reasons.

By reasons, I do not mean that all should be sound, but even the unsound reasons find easier applications in today's world.

> *Every word that proceeds from a man's mouth is subject to investigation since man, the weird and the wizened, have devised means of saying many things even with one word and at the same time.*

However, I must warn that at the rate the world is going, that no man or institution can be trusted, it is still humanity that will suffer grave consequences when no man can be trusted.

Life and business will experience bitter pains and misery when trust perishes from among men.

Taking a man at his word is little of trust and more of simplicity. Not being able to unravel the secret of a man's word is not enough reason to believe him.

The beauty and strength of the arts can only be discovered in the practice.

> *The mind does not give the mouth that which it does not have in stock.*

Explosive expression is a sign of tolerance exhaustion but this is not enough for a man not to develop his capacity to contain the forces of life.

You cannot be an artist with a small brain!

You have to expand your memory capacity and arm yourself with options.

You have to step up your ops and move ahead of the group to be able to see before it comes.

You need to create enough space so you can play around. To be the real master in your field, you have to play on bigger pitch.

It is often hard to find the right words to express thoughts and this is often why the wise refuse to talk and the unwitty let anything go,; but the man that makes talk his game must have abundance of words to play around. You may need to consider the time, the place, the mood and the trigger before you can understand the word.

> *In a world where knowledge is limited, right or wrong is only a function of perception.*

Evidence is everything!

Evidence is the backbone of every sound persuasion and false evidence is the soul of strong deception.

A good artist must understand the beauty of words and the burden of proof.

105

MENTALITY II

There is an important art that links the form to the function.

They call it genetics but a fanatical adherence to the genetical speculations may seek to debase the idea of identity.

The environment makes the man as much as the man makes the environment, but it is indeed difficult to assent to the idea that there is a relationship between people who superficially look identical and their inbuilt mechanism of action in terms of intelligence and instincts.

Those who look alike often think and act alike,

but this in itself is hard to believe due to amazing variations. Character is a matter of disposition and those who assume criminal disposition often take to criminal tendencies and tendencies control thoughts.

Thought and tendencies may exchange position one coming before the other in whatever order, but this does not change the relationship between them.

It is natural blessing to look like Venus, and whatever you resemble has some relationship to a pre-existing similarity. Every character has a predecessor considering the ages of human existence but there has never been identical humans.

If you can have the luck of seeing the devil, be strict with those who possess his identity.

Nature has taken time to draw signs to explain inbuilt mechanism. Some are found on the face, others in their acts. When you find the kind of structure you have never seen before; take time to know what is special about them.

Do not ignore signs, wherever it may be written, it is at your own peril.

Live like one driving on the high way, do not ignore road signs.

Check out, you would be surprise there is no much difference between them, both priests and strumpets when they look alike.

The only difference is the feelings of fear and freedom and in the same state, they are agonists.

A pig can be clean as long as it can't make it to the mud,
and many can continue to be holy for want of opportunity.

Thanks to deception and persuasion, the characters in the world would have made the world to explode.

At times the only wrong thing a girl ever does to deserve the place of a courtesan is simply being beautiful. Who has ever asked her hand that never wanted to succeed? If she bends to every pressure, is she not of easy virtue? But if she does not bend to yours, would you respect her and let her be?

Anybody can be deceived; and if you end up being deceived by one of these, do not hit yourself too hard, we all have desires that can be used against us. Whatever is known about you in life can be used against you, and so you may know, no secret about you is known to you alone.

But if I can tell you the winning card, stay clean as much as you can! It is an herculean task cleaning your dirty linens and bad records once it has been thrown to the public.

106

CONTENTMENT

The soul of happiness is the sense of contentment.

No human being ever exist without anything.

There is this story of a man who thought all is over with him, he went to the bush and hang himself. Then came another man half naked, and finding this hanging man on fine trousers, removed it and put on himself and went his way thanking God.

People who take time out to look at themselves in solemn ponder will discover amazing occurrences and vast magnanimity of nature and the supernatural gesture.

It is not a sign of good rationale to blame people for whatever state one finds himself for those that would never survive, nature had already taken away.

If nature then has permitted that you still exist, then there is a way you can make it

even to the top, if only you take out time to search around you for this way.

Good things do not come out of the evil way, but at times, you may have to step on people's toes before you can make it beyond their barrier.

A man's misfortunes in life is not a statement of the errors of his ways, bad things do happen to good people on this side heaven.

Somewhere along the line of your daily endeavors, your interest will collide with another man's interest; don't be surprised at this, you are not the only one who deserves good things, others do also.

The world is a market place, as there are many sellers, so are there many buyers. If you can pay the price, you will always have what you want.

> *Success is never gotten, it is earned. If you have anything of value to sell, then there are people who need it to buy; look for them until you find them.*

If you can realize that you worked, and as a result you have had something to show for it, be a normal man and be happy about it for not many have been able to experience this.

> *If what you have at hand does not give you satisfaction, what you want to have may never satisfy you.*

To every question is an answer and in every answer, questions, except in the minds of simple men.

More haste, less speed and the more we get the more we want.

The poor man will swear by the gods, that if he could afford to be as rich as the other, he would never want again.

But he forgets to look at himself, that he is rich even in poverty, yet still envying the positions of others.

Don't be a fool, there is nothing that you will eat that your hand will stick in your mouth forever; it will come out, and soon, you will want again.

The victims of choice may never make one, for even the best is only subject to time.

The beautiful ones are not yet born was the right thing to say, but this does not excuse a man from deciding on one, for he will never witness the most of all beauty in his lifetime.

We can assent a bird at hand is worth two in the bush, but only very few people have taken time to realize they have a bird to hold unto at all.

If you keep telling a monkey that it is beautiful, soon it will grab the idea and begin to see itself in the same light.

Indecision is the worst of all indiscipline; it makes you susceptible to hurts and regrets.

Even when decision hurts, a great mind will find a reason to be happy he made a choice.

From the very moment you took a decision, whatever prompted you, it was already too late to regret.

107

PERCEPTION

It is funny how we think, each of the other person. I always applaud the sense of fear.

> *By fear, men have taken to telling the truth, afraid that attempts to say the things that are not true may be discovered and disgraced.*

You cannot deny the effect that the presence of people have upon your life, nor can you deny that some of the things you do are either because they are present or absent, whether this is real or imagine.

The fear of the LORD, it is written, is the beginning of wisdom and many people would never be the same if only they had their way.

Human actions proceed from thoughts.

Even in the face of provocation, we can only apart inadequate deliberation.

The way we think of the other person influences how we act towards them.

> *If you by any means knew your son will be president in his time, you will do everything in your power to give him the needed training.*

But you do not feel that highly about him, and very soon that is the same way he will be seeing himself and falling unto drugs. The right words spoken to a man at the right time gives him a vision of the proper way in life.

> *Men often think women have no brains; women feel it is the other way round, more that men have no minds.*

Although this logic may be lexically erroneous, a non-utilization of one's possession is as bad as not having it at all. Why should a woman who, with all natural endowment and ability, yet resigns to feeding from the droppings of a man's pocket, not considering her ability to make a hundred times of that still upholding her dignity, be thought to be having a brain? There are many ways we throw away our dignity in knowledge and sound reasoning, taking to the path of tricks and deception, but how long do these things last?

Your dignity is your person, without which you are either a cadaver or a slave.

Thinking of a man to be having no mind is sequitur to your feeling. This is how every slave thinks of a master who wants the maximal utilization of the labor of his slave.

A slave is what you make yourself, simply for not utilizing your potentials. We all need each other, but this does not mean that we cannot be ourselves.

Nobody will ever make you what you are not willing to make yourself.

> *You are more important than the services you render, but until you make the services depend on you, others will turn the table the other way round.*

Albeit the foregone, men and women do not like telling the truth of themselves to each other, for fear this would bias their perception of the other.

Even fear should be able to warn them that the truth will be discovered someday even to their disgrace and that, at a wrong time and in a wrong place.

This is how much we seek to deceive each other, accepting the lies in place of truth

Only those with the third eye can see the truth in their women.

Those who cannot afford a third eye can connect the vision of their spectators; they see more than you can think of. An average man will paint his neighbor black, but if you are wise, hang around only people who are willing to paint you in bright colors; this is your winning card in the game of life and living.

When a man tells you he is watching you, run away, he will never see anything good in you in the long run. There is no man on this earth that is dirt free; any man who digs around will always find something hidden somewhere.

108

DIGNITY

It is only a disciplined man who can say no to an evil profit.

> *Why would a toad not find itself in the stomach of a snake when it does not make holes, yet always seeking to live in one?*

The agents of lure do not hold in their hands the things that cannot trip you.

The fact that the horse has always been dragging the cart does not mean that the cart should in turn try to drag the horse.

In fact, the horse and the cart do not exchange position, but the horse may make the choice of a rider.

> *Who will not marry a princess, the heiress to the throne of envy, though she is indeed a monster?*

This is the way men run away from the realities of their non-utilization of their potentials to survival.

We seek means in our undertaking instead of the end in themselves.

Men accept disgrace upon themselves in the quest to overcome their own disgrace. Seeking the most beautiful to overcome our ugliness and the rich to overcome our poverty. This in itself is not a wrong thing to do but only that we have in the course of this, enslaved ourselves to those whose dignity should make them our own servants.

However this may sound, it does not mean there is an evil in services;

in fact, we all live on the services we render to other people; that's why we get paid without which you are a thief, reaping where you did not sow

Indeed, every man should establish himself in a line of service and get paid for his daily toil.

Instead of strategizing to position yourself for favor, improve on your services and attract for yourself a bigger pay, soon you will get to the top with your dignity intact.

A monster is a monster no matter the title we attach to them.

Attachments do not make the substance

beyond what they are, except to the mind of a simple man which you can avoid being reckoned as one.

Nobody should be a servant of another man with his dignity as a person, but those who neglect their potentials and find themselves in servitude should not expect a better treatment. Indeed, with one talent you can get to the sky, even while others are blessed with ten of their best. You need not to complain or hide.

> *No bird will soar in the skies until its spreads its wings; and*
> *no talent will multiply until you put same to proper use.*

There are many treasures to be discovered when a man digs deep enough in his back yard.

Only a man can call a spade a spade and not some insipient devil spoon.

The worst that can happen to you is for you to be known as Mr. 'yes Sir', they will not seize to make you a factotum.

These two letters word, "No", is what those who lord over you do not like hearing, but it is what you must gather your courage to say, when it is the best to say.

Even in your weakness is strength, find this and stand tall upon it.

Even though the snail is known to be slow, it cannot be swallowed by a snake.

109

GLORY

Glory is a grace bestowed on those who try to do their very best in their undertakings in life.

We may choose to wonder why glory is not a right, but we can realize that not every burden constitutes a cross.

The cross is the means to glory but when the right cross is carried by the wrong person, it constitutes only a mere load. Many people seek to bring disgrace upon their glory, and many others are reduced from grace to grass every day.

Every position of honor is a seat of temptation and

he who feels the weight of his power will be the very first to fall.

To whom much is given is much expected, and the sun will never dance in the day without the observance of man, for up there, there are many eyes looking its way.

The path to glory is paved with many misery; only those with strong will and good character make it to the finish line.

Many other people in the world are fleeing from the cross every day.

Many other people believe in the beam of fate but a wise man will not wait to be blessed by chance.

Chance itself does not favor a mind that is not prepared for it, but if you are thus prepared, what are you waiting for?

All the lights will never turn green, so take the next available chance and hope for the better.

There are no short cuts to the crown without the cross.

The idea of the wrong cross may sound illusive but you must bear in mind that the wrong labor will never pay the right wage. You can recall that

Christ was not the only man who died on the cross, but he was the only crucified and glorified.

The cross was the destiny of Christ, the others got there because they were thieves.

The only right cross for a man is the price of who he wants to be as related to who he is.

If who you want to be has no relationship with who you are, you may spare yourself the task of vain labor or you may just go ahead in useless dissipation of energy, after all, you are not the first person to do this.

The cross is not as light as the mass of the wood, there are invisible attachments.

Many forces fight against you even with the cross on your shoulder, the world does not really want you to wear the crown!

The urge to deny the cross is the strongest opposition to the crown,

and the enemy of your progress may not stop at this, but may go ahead to promise wage without work.

Those who seek to die a valiant death never die without the crown on their head, but those who desert the ship in the storm will miss the calm ahead.

We live in a world where the right is constantly being persecuted by the wrong, darkness is attacking every appearance of light because of the evil of their way, men of religion using terror to defend their error. It is not enough to plan to be good, you must develop the strength to overcome the forces of evil.

110

LIFE II

Life on earth is not an end in itself, but a means to an end. If life on earth were to be an end, it would be the most useless endeavor to any advocate of reason.

How do you feel, realizing you came with nothing and will go with nothing; that you are busy about everything but will take nothing along in your exit; why would one even struggle without any guarantee of a longer life?

Pondering on life itself can be very frustrating, though all these struggles will one day amount to nothing. If there is no point to prove in life, then every achievement is useless altogether since nothing follows a man to his grave, that is, if he is lucky to even have a grave.

You hope to be remembered, but those who went ahead of you how many have been remembered?

> *And even if you were to be remembered, of what benefit is memory to the dead? Just do the best you can for humanity, favors are not meant to be returned.*

Your father was the poorest man in your village, yet you are today a rich man to be reckoned with.

You deprive others of means of livelihood in other to heap billions for your children, do you not think you are assisting them to make a useless time in their living? If you keep for your children everything they would need in their lifetime, what would they be doing with their own time of life?

You can see the world as a field of introduction

and a farmer does not introduce his crop into the field without a purpose.

Time and purpose cannot be separated.

There is time for every purpose and a purpose for every time. When it does not follow the proper appointment, life can become so useless and frustrating.

Of all the seeds that were introduced into the field, it is certain that some will be selected.

Whatever constitutes the criteria for the selection is best known to the farmer, but it is certain that he will not fail to give all the seeds enabling environment to justify his judgment.

If the farmer should be unjust in his dealing with seeds, then all the seeds should gang up against him and destroy him, but

justice is more powerful than a disarming smile.

Whatever remains to be settled is an understanding between the crop and the farmer, and between man and his creator. Whatever other criteria will be used for the selection, I know the farmer will never ignore the crop that produced the highest yield, from which the farmer hopes to make more profit from his daily toil.

After selection, there is sure to be the planting in the permanent field for the experience of an eternal blossom. And it is not good to make mistake in the selection less you will have to select twice.

If nature is the one who will do the selection, then tricks will not set for I know nature as one who does not make mistakes in his dealings.

While you live and dine, try and realize that this is only a means, look forward to the end.

111

SURVIVAL

The servant should not execute the master in aversion of the rigors of his training.

It is said that

> *those who kill others in order to succeed, will have death*
> *waiting as sentinel at the post of their success.*

Sudden jumps make sudden falls and the pain is the price of the gain. In the world,

> *hard times do not last, but hard men do.*

And when the goings gets tough, the tough gets going. No retreat, no surrender, forward ever backward never.

Strongmen are bound to survive and exercise is the source of strength.

Survival is continuous, as a critical look at life itself will show life is a disaster; you will always need to survive if you stay alive; the living are the survivors of the disaster called 'life'.

You learn to speak by speaking and to lead by leading.

What you are is more important than what you want to be and you can be whatever you want to be if only you seek to fully utilize what you are.

Language starts from the alphabet and every sky scraper is built on a foundation.

The world is a stage on which only those who are able to push above the level of confusion can find themselves on a visible horizon.

If David had avoided the lion, he would not possibly have been able to confront Goliath.

> *Every stage in the drama of life is a preparatory for the next line of action, and every obstacle you avoid on the course of your progress will sum against you at the point of your success.*

A man who skips his lessons will always be in need of assistance at the critical moments of his struggle.

Challenges are an inalienable part of life procession; it all depends on how you look at them and the way you respond to them.

Whichever way you choose to see it, they are capable of getting you bitter or better progressing or frustrating depending on whether you see them as stepping stones or stumbling blocks. The whole lifespan is like a thick forest that exists in between you and your destiny.

You have to clear this forest and enjoy of whatever you find in it while preserving that which is worth preserving for some rainy day.

You may choose to jump over some parts of the forest, but do not be surprise, the very key to your room is hidden in that very part, so leave no stone unturned.

Many people have jumped this way to arrive at their destined house but yet cannot enter, simply because they do not have the right keys which they would have gotten the right way.

Life will always continue to unfold new opportunities every day, but only those who are prepared will ever be able to take one of these.

Short cuts are often the wrong path.

112

DEATH III

There is something special about the hour of death, which summarizes the time of man's life.

The premonition of the life after death falls on men at the point of transition

> *While it is okay to take all the advantages that there is in life, it is also wise to consider another period of helplessness after strength.*

For now you are strong and can carry your weight and you forget someone did all that for you sometimes ago, and soon you will need others to be doing it for you.

Two expressions are often found in the faces of death men, smiles and frowns, with or without tears. Whatever this may stand for, it is a picture of the state of his new surroundings.

Our road ends were we have our homes and at the end of the means of life, there is an end that is justified.

It is pertinent to ask, when the cool hands of death fall on you, will you shed tears of joy or sadness?

Whatever comes and goes in life, there is an end that is proportional and real, deception cannot change nor can persuasion brand. It is said that

> *it is not only folly to deny the existence of God, it is also wise to acknowledge his presence among men.*

There are things you would never be able to explain in life but this in itself is not enough reason for you to succumb to deceit. Good and evil shall continue to be done on earth and their instruments shall ever be man. You may choose who to serve.

The end will always justify the means and

the acknowledgement of the temporary nature of life should be enough caution for a reasonable mind.

It is indeed a pity that we brag about everything when indeed we do not have anything. Everything in this life is borrowed and no man knows when the owner will come to take back His possession.

113

REASONING

In whatever you choose to do, try and think first before you act.

It will be a blessing to you if you can let your thought sleep for a night before you transform them into words and actions.

> *If you are still excited about the idea tomorrow as you are*
> *excited about it today, then you would be partially justified*
> *it could be the right thing to do.*

As a matter of fact, every human head is always thinking, the only difference between one and the other is the quality of what you think of and the product.

Every item of thought that is allowed to be processed by the mind will certainly yield an end product, desirable or undesirable, consciously or unconsciously; it is garbage in, garbage out!

Though many people think, very few of this number can be said to reason.

By reason you compare, contrast and then streamline.

Of this few that can be said to reason, only very few of them can act to their reasoning due to their vulnerability to the pressures of life situations.

You must understand that any situation that come your way comes with enough force to secure your attention, this is the force that you must fight back to recover your senses.

Reason can be enslaved to emotion and action can also proceed from reasons based on individual sophistication.

In whatever you have to do, let your reasons surpass pressure or you will dance to the rhythms of emotions.

One of the greatest mistakes in life is to find yourself wallowing in the messy fantasies of other men.

Two good heads are better than one but two bad heads is a disaster.

You may wonder how it is possible that reasons supersede emotions, but it is a simple thing to do. Just ask yourself why, in action and adamancy and when you say 'because', put another "why" after it.

Finding answers to questions and questions in answers is all but mental business, but it is the soul of hitch free actions.

Emotion is a sound music, playing at the right time and presenting visible virtual consequences.

It is easy to yield since it scarcely results in unattractive figures even when we would have blocked the procession by attaining the proper knowledge of our situation.

The fact that other people hold their views does not mean you should not have your own view.

It is good to use the opinions of others to streamline your own position but do not wait for others to say what you have to do.

You may trust in others but this is not enough reason for you not to trust in yourself.

Do not ever lack an opinion either of others or of yourself.

You are the only person you know best.

114

ATTRIBUTION

Attribution is the worst enemy of solution to human problems.

Develop your own mind and do not live on borrowed opinions.

Understand that others can be wrong, and do not abandon your opinion without a clear conviction; assumption is the mother of all fuckups, it is said.

Arrogance is the first born of ignorance and insolence is his twin brother, and when they grow up, pride will be their vocation.

It is either man changes things to suit him or things will change man to suit them. When the crooked cannot be made straight, then the straight must go or at least appear crooked to survive.

Man is powerful against adverse circumstances of his life as well as susceptible to their effect, whichever way he chooses to run being a sole responsibility of the individual man.

There is no alternative to knowledge in life, even when its acquisition is a levodextrous phenomenon.

The human mind accepts as much as it can from the society yet until man realizes the effect of his society on him, before he starts to filter based on what he wants.

Man can only be something in the world, and not everything. He needs to accept something from the society to enable him attain this and not anything.

The very last person we blame for our misfortunes in life, the very cause of our misfortunes, is our very self. Undeveloped potentials is synonymous to poverty, untrained muscles a friend to laziness, restricted vision as good as blindness. Diligence, derived from hard work and determination, is the mother of good fortune.

The lands will never fail to give back what it had been given nor will the seeds refuse to grow if you plant them in season. No man can avoid the fruit of his labor and indeed the natural world system has been set to pay in right proportion, the wages as the circumstances of his life may determine.

The knowledge of the consequence of the action you are about to take is important before you attempt taking them.

If the price of your actions is what you cannot pay today, do not deceive yourself of paying it anyway or anyhow tomorrow.

If you are not convinced, then ask your elders who took your kind of stand and they will tell you it never worked for them. Emotion is a drunk driver, if you allow yourself to be driven by same into insane decisions, your eyes will clear in the face of reality, when it all will seem to have evaporated and you look deserted and derailed from the bridge into the bottom of the sea below.

You can only choose your actions but not the consequences, it is the consequence that will choose you. It is either you pay for the consequence, or it will take from you by force, even that which you needed most.

Only sow the seed which fruit you can contain.

115

LOVE VI

Love is a supernatural encounter between natural beings. Love has always been though lovers come and go.

Love is built on expectations and even in an unconditional condition, there is bound to be something in sight.

> *Any love that is founded on nothing will never cross the first bridge of adversity.*

Love is a beautiful boat for two on the high sea of life, it will never survive the storm without an anchor to hold.

Whichever way you see it, on the high sea of life, it is safer in the boat of love, without which you are stranded, frustrated or sinking beneath the waves.

Being between natural beings, love never runs smooth on its course, but with frictions at irregular intervals.

One prevalent problem between lovers is their inability to see the difference that exists in the other person as well as the variation that is bound to be, between their expectations and what they actually get from the other person.

Every person seeks as much as possible to hide the ugly part of his life in order not to scare competitors, while hot cakes may display foul camouflage to scare predators and pests.

Men and women pass judgment on the opposite sex immediately they come in contact, arousing the disgust and desire. While the married mind may be relaxed by the impending circumstances, youngsters get super excited by possibilities.

This is how it goes James, but if you were to ask me, I would say that

> *I find more love in a perfect reconciliation than in a first sight affection.*

A perfect reconciliation is the employment of a Divine act in a supernatural course.

Man is an animal of change, always tending to explore other avenues in search of greener pastures.

I always watch with dismay when men and women take oaths before the altar, lying before God and man without a single sign of remorse; if such oaths where so easy to keep, then no man will go to court to enforce the love he professes.

But the oath is even better because it entangles him with some obligation, without which you are just like the television set he bought the other day.

But would that this also be included in the marriage oath; "LOOK BEFORE PURCHASE, NO REFUND AFTER PAYMENT; NO RETURN AFTER PURCHASE".

> *In order for man not to be tied down by a particular range, he always seeks gaps in the fence to escape without blame.*

When a man is determined to do a thing, he will always find reasons to do what he wants to do whatever others think. The same when a man is determined not to do a thing.

> *Every human has got enough weaknesses to be discarded, so it is nothing when you discard another in a hurry because of his weakness.*

Because the first sight does not afford an opportunity to consider the infirmities, the ability to compromise this after realization is what constitutes the super love.

Falling in love is the first evidence of lust. Love does not fall, but stands together committed to each other no matter what.

Men and women are not what you see, but be happy if you can still love them after you have known who they are. Know what is important to you in a man or a woman; and when you have found the one who has this, you have made a good choice; you will never find every virtue in one person.

We make love that it may make us and through bends and mends, we will run a straight course.

116

HOPE II

Hope is the archangel that guards sane minds.

> *The last thing a man looses in life is hope, the gap between beings and beasts,*

the anchor that keeps life in position when the storms rage in fury upon the high seas of life.

Circumstances come and circumstances go but life continues. Of what necessity is it to live and see your death rather than dying at once? This is where hope is gone and hell lets loose its content.

The feeling that it shall never be well in the future, either real or imagined is the worst sensation on the life of humans.

Hope is the root of peace.

No matter what a man faces in life, the only thing he needs is the conviction that tomorrow will be a better day.

Man does not want to be told that he shall never have what he wants, but only the way he can get it even if it will take time for it to come to pass.

I know of a man who was given a life term in jail, ten years later I visited him and felt pity for him, and I asked him what keeps him going, he said to my surprise, "I know that one day I shall be free".

> *The best way to get a man in order, is to give him hope in the direction of his thoughts.*

The enduring people of the world are the hopeful ones even when all hope is gone.

Despair, is the root of violence.

The best way to get a man into a violent behavior is to enlighten him of the hopeless nature of his situation. Desperation can be depressively or anxiously motivated. Violence can be towards an innocent person, any person believed to be the cause of the hopeless situation, or towards self out of the realization that one cannot change the situation to suit his state.

If only men realized that the world is ruled on the principles of cause and effect, action and consequence, then there would be no need to be despaired about the future.

Those who sow good seeds should expect good fruit, either soon or delayed, while those who sowed evil seeds should not expect anything at variance with evil.

You absolutely do not need to be violent about the fruit of your labor as two wrongs do not make a right.

If you never sowed, then expect no yield.

I have watched people deceived of fat sums of money trying to claim prizes they are said to have won in games they never played, what a pity! But realizing you should sow is an indication that today is a better day.

Before you regret tomorrow again, you should have sowed today.

Nature never cheats, you will reap what you sow or you should sow what you reaped.

117

SERVICE III

I would say do not call anybody your master, but it is obvious some people had gone this road ahead of you and can get you up to them if only you co-operate.

The highway of life is only traversed once; people know what they have met with in life and not what they are going to meet, so it is better to learn the principles.

The easier way to get to the top is to borrow from people who have gone half way, and a child will build easily if only the father had laid the foundation.

Man is born potential slave to two opposite forces of which he will have to choose one or the other chooses him. Man either chooses good or evil chooses him, knowledge or ignorance chooses him, freedom or slavery choose him and success or failure chooses of him.

Between man and these forces,

A master is a master and a slave is a slave.

The master and his slave do not exchange position though the master will have to Carter for the needs of his slave in order to sustain the efficiency of his service.

This should make you happy if you see yourself a master, but unfortunately, things have not always been the same in this changing world and times.

It is in the character of every man to seek to be the one at the top, to seek to be the one to be worshipped by all, but I tell you my friend, when you have survived and you can stand alone, break the bonds and live free; there is nothing as sweet in life like to be a free man in your own world.

When you have attained a dependable status, men will depend on you; if you become their lord, it is not a crime, just don't look down on yourself.

Life is smarter than any man, there is room for overtaking in life.

For you to remain the master, you must keep fit and pushing without relent without which you will be overtaken.

Do not just get angry at a man who proves to be smarter, that's life. If you are not going up, you are going down.

Even birds will fall from the skies if they do not struggle to stay afloat.

If you do not serve this very master, you have already submitted yourself to the service of the other.

There is no sitting on the fence in the affairs of life.

If you do not learn, then you are a learner forever.

Although we seek so much to master our slavery to the forces of life in other to contain them, he who refuses to serve, is a servant forever.

Tricks do not work, double sidedness is accidental and fatal, while circumstance is excusable.

A great slave is one who learns about his master in his service, and it is this that will master his master into his service.

Do not depend on what you do, rather let what you do depend on you.

As a matter of fact, in life, any good servant will soon be in a position to higher his poor master.

It is better to choose than to be chosen. Choose what you want to do and do what you love to do.

Give your service to men, but work for yourself.
We all serve ourselves from the service we render to other men.

Your talents and your gifts are the assets the world has got to progress, discover the best of you and give in exchange for what you want in life.

118

MATERIALISM

You would better understand the value of a thing, if you were to borrow it from a friend. The things we have in/on us do not so much count for us as the ones we yearn to have.

This is not because they do not count in themselves, but because they have been with us and have been regarded common as sense.

> *It would be virtuous to understand the values of the things that we have, for only in this will we be able to put the right things in their right place.*

Imagine how much you would have to pay for one of these things had they not been given to you freely.

It would serve the course for a man not to throw anything away, but for the fact that some possessions are so useless that they only consume precious space in their keeping.

Do not throw your things away simply because you feel it should be thrown away, but do not fail to discard of any of your possession if you know that it should be discarded.

> *Many mysteries of your possession are revealed at the brink of your loosing.*

This is not that you should continue to heap things for their mysteries to reveal or that you first throw them away trying to discover their mysteries through that, but simply that you may *bear in mind when your possessions appear useless to you, that they are not as useless as you feel.*

There are some things you cannot stop from happening if you are the type that likes heaping things.

The more things you heap, the less control you have over them and the more visible you are to predators; termites and rodents, both human and non-human.

But if you are wise, you will develop a thick skin like the elephant, this way you will be tough for the claws of a tiger.

You make your things what it makes you.

Do not fail to change whatever you can change for the better, as well as resisting a bad possession to change you simply because you cannot change it.

Decide the fate of things before things decide your fate.

But in doing this, you have to be extra careful for diamonds can be found in the mud and stars can be found buried in scars. Life is not about how much you get from it, but how well you use the little you have to the greater good.

If what you have is put to better use, you would not bother so much as to the much you never have.

Do not fail to understand that what you heap for the next generation may not be relevant to them in their time; we live in a changing world, the only thing children need to be great is good training, a good name as a legacy and a better society; not stolen riches.

119

LOVE VII

Only man creates chances, chances do not make a man. No man has ever had enough for seasons, but from the much that a man has, his will distributes.

Life is about give and take, it is said, but wise men only rush to give while allowing gifts to rush after them.

> *To whatever a man loves, he enslaves himself and objects of love do not disgust the mind of their lover.*

Things are given to man freely in due season but for man to force this things on himself, he has to pay a price.

There is so much talk about love and giving recently that some have begun to think that when the word "love" is mentioned, gifts will begin to flow like a broken pipe.

> *It may be wise never to go into a love affair when you are not in the mood to sacrifice.*

I talk about love as about life because they suck from the same breast. When all your life is about the greater pay, just about what you can get and not what you can give and not the greater good, then you are just another mistake that life has made, another burden that the world has to bear.

All of life is a grand love affair, to give and to have the love of others; you will never understand the magic of life until you begin to give to it.

Love does not survive between straight poles, but better with flexible rods. While you hope to get something from any love affair, it is pertinent to consider spending something that you may never get back. It is obvious you may get no true love if you hold stiff to your stand. You simply have to put some things apart and especially your pride.

A better person to love is the one that considers oneself not worthy of your love; if you doubt my saying, ask from the Christ, but the proud and arrogant is a mine field, a disaster waiting to happen at the slightest provocation.

You may have to give out of nothing, but do not give to your displeasure.

A valiant man may have to beg in love as well a strong one cry.

> *You will on many occasions compromise your stand if you wish to understand your love. You may have to be the offended and the repentant at the same time, just so you can give peace a chance.*

You may have to tell her a little of your secrets in good timing, if you want to know all the secrets about her.

You may have at times to accept death, if you wish to preserve the life of your love.

You will, above all have to accept the losses that there may be, if only you want to gain.

But a man who is too careful of losses, is not worthy of any gain.

120

JEALOUSY

Jealousy is the basic instinct of rich potentials.

It is nature to admire, human to desire, brave to compete and great that it should be no other person than you.

It is at times good that it is you that failed despite the much effort you put in to ensure a win, for had it mean it happened to others, you would have found a thousand reason to blame them for their failure.

One problem of man and signals is that of proper interpretation.

However consistent nature has been in giving its signals so that it does not confuse any human beings or beasts, it appears man is the least to comprehend though he claims the better off with some bigger brain.

The signal that makes you realize that you are poor does not say that you should always be poor.

The signal that makes a perpetual fool is that which deceives him of his strength in wisdom while he is swimming in the spring of folly.

The very reason a man's ignorance is revealed to him is that he should get up and work very fast to acquire knowledge.

Jealousy is a natural tool of action.

It is very normal to be jealous of some attainments of a superior degree and by this instinct, work to get it.

The proper interpretation of the signal to jealousy is the arousal of a greater intensity of work and the determination to make it at all cost.

My little book of piety teaches that whatever a man seeks, that he finds. I talk of jealousy as if of envy, whatever turns your stomach when you watch others going ahead of you whether it is real or imagined.

People work to get what they have and there is no way you can work the way they do without getting what they have gotten if only you believe in the natural laws.

You will realize you can have anything in life, if you start searching for them where they can be found.

Albeit the realities of actions and proportional reactions, it is real that a greater number of people with great potentials based on their ability to desire great things, simply sit to think and thin.

Wishes do not make horses and choices are not made on single alternative. **Life will never give you many options, only some opportunities here and there, some of which are not worth taking except at your peril.**

Jealousy without work is a tool of mental slavery.

There is a way you can avoid this; simply work your way to the top of your field, and you will no more need to be seeking great things, instead, great things will be begging to be allowed your way.

Beggars wish they had a horse while horses wish they were owned by a king.

You will never have to struggle hard to have the things that wish they belong to you.

If you do not have so much to pay for those things you want, then save the much you have for the ones that want you; these ones will be easier to get.

You can avoid being a beggar, if you seek and follow the path that finds the throne.

Square pegs shall never fit into round holes. You either round the peg or square the holes, whichever is easier, without which you get nowhere.

121

GREATNESS II

Man changes according to the changes in his living conditions. The positive change cannot be guaranteed nor can the negative change be assured.

Environmental change changes man and human change changes the environment.

> *As the changes on the inside affect the outside, so does the changes on the outside affect the inside.*

Religion came to change the hopelessness in human living. Man accepts the hope, fashioning it in a way that changes his religion to suit him.

> *There is a difference between the god you created and the God who created you; one you can send at your will, the other you must obey.*

Heraclitus was not wrong when he postulated the primordial substance of the universe to be change, one of the forces that ensure life and progression.

It is folly for life to resist change, forgetting that it is change that created life, and change that continues to sustain the life of man.

Selfishness and greed draw a map for change to follow, but change has grown beyond this, following its own way to accomplish the predetermined.

Every man that prays tries to use God for one thing or the other, but God is also looking for a man willing for God to use him to bless.

Great minds set the pace in life,

great acts beat the clock while great people beat the age.

There is this one character that is not lacking in great men; their ability to take quick decisive steps.

> *To see quickly, decide quickly and act quickly is a winning trait in this world of abounding uncertainties.*

There are acts that fit into the time and every philosopher is a fitting peg in the hole of his time.

> *The post contemporary standard of religious living is magnanimity in ingratitude and goodness towards a proven unworthy faction.*

This is the pace, the most that we so much need for the world to go on.

Gratitude has always been expected from the recipients of noble acts, but it is obvious that the rate has fallen in the present day.

If you then can continue generosity in negligence of the ingratitude of men, yours is the world, and the sky is your limit.

It is said to be folly to be wise where ignorance is found to be bliss and wise to be grateful in the midst of ungrateful people.

What does not come, may never come, but it is not enough reason for life not to continue.

A lizard should continue to be a lizard and a chameleon, a chameleon. But

> *A lizard may pretend a chameleon if this constitutes the spelling of survival.*

It might even decide to cut its tail, but it will certainly not be able to jump like a frog.

If you can trust yourself when every other person distrusts you, if you can show you love when every other person seems to hate you, if you can continue to do good when all you get in return is evil, yours too is the world and the sky, your limit.

The measure of a man's greatness is not far from the strength of his power and the extent of his influence.

Power, this is what you get when you keep going higher against all odds and negative realities.

122

PRETENCE

Pretension is an important art for human survival. It is an important way that humans try to adapt to the living environment or societal pressure which constitutes part of the higher bombardment of the human life and wellbeing.

> *To go this way in pretense to the other makes you free from suspicion even in the acts of evil.*

A common sense will tell you that the good has nothing to pretend about, but I can tell you that as long as the good has something in him that the evil desires, he has already become a target, and needs to cover his trails.

Every human finds a reason to pretend in some of the aspects of his life even when it shall be revealed to his shame.

While some sorts of pretense can lead you to the other side of the road, others are simply non Sequitur, treating the important things as unimportant and the unimportant things as important.

> *When a servant of God pretends before man, is he deceiving himself or his God.*

This is the kind of things we should consider while choosing our actions, that we may never sacrifice the important thing in the temple of the unimportant.

A student pretending before his teacher, finds himself comfortable, and praises himself for the mastery of the art even when he is sacrificing his knowledge, the very essence of his studentship.

The simplest thing for a pretender to understand is that pretense lasts as long as a borrowed life can be comfortable to the borrower.

The arts done in pretense suit like a borrowed rope with loose ends and tight angles.

It is good to pretend to the unimportant in order to take the important, and not striving to please what does not constitute the headline of your mission statement.

A pretender should understand that he is avoiding that aspect of his life that should better have been confronted, disconnected or strengthen.

The greatest kindness you can do to evil is exposure; and light is the revealer of the foolishness of the secrets of darkness.

> *The fact that you are yet to be caught in the act of evil does not make you a good man, but only sparing you an evil title.*

A man living in pretense is like a woman dancing calypso on a mine field; soon she would not be able to dance again for the rest of her life when the mine has chopped off her limbs.

You are what you are, whatever the people may be thinking of you notwithstanding.

123

LIBERTY

Liberty constitutes a sweet sensation to the human mind to his own good, even in the art of his doing evil.

Nobody wants to be hindered by another person, even the worst of all fools.

Freedom is so inherent that even when the mind is deranged, the greatest desire of the insane is not to be disturbed even while he is wallowing in a refuse dump.

Many things can a man do, much causing harm to other human beings.

The confusion of instinct to inspiration and the urge to action makes the consequent act a child of the chance.

The best of all reasons does not surface the minds of humans, but a good reason will always present restrictions.

Knowledge is the virtue of all actions for a sound taking of it does not present advantages without caution of the impending disadvantages.

To be free to do anything at any time can be demanded by a simple mind, but it should be understood that

every predator is a prey to another predator.

A straying sheep will always come back with a belly full of grass, but how long before it finds itself in the belly of a cat?

A tree that wants to live long stands under the Kola tree and unity is the strength of the broom.

There are two important securities for well-being; a running spring, and a well that never dries.

> *Freedom is the most destructive of all possessions yet it is the yearning of all creatures on earth. Man is not abnormal in his zest for freedom, for it is the hangover of his era of wandering life.*

Let everyman beware, for if all men should be given their freedom, then the world will be worse than a jungle. Thomas Hobbes reminds me that "man is born free, but is always in chain" and I add that

> *the chain is necessary, for it changes a beast into a being. The chains itself does not cure the madness of men, it only stops them from causing harm to others and themselves.*

The freedom of man should be only within the circumference of his chain and beyond this, he is a terror to all other animals in their chain. To let free of everyman is to initiate another era of cannibalism that is characterized by the

> *undefined theory of survival of the fittest that has no criteria for fitness,*

not in broad shoulders nor in tachy muscles.

Freedom can make you, it can also maim you. It can make you a victor as well as a victim.

When you give freedom to a child, be sure you give him protection as well.

One problem I have with the advocates of liberty is that they struggle so hard to earn what they do not plan how to spend. It is far easier to earn freedom; the greater task is how to spend it properly.

Every hunter is a hunted.

124

SAVINGS

If I were to choose were to be after my life here on earth, I would choose the heavenly kingdom. In heaven, I shall eat without cooking, drink without fetching, drive without fueling and be pleased without working. Even here on earth, these kinds of things happen, but only to those who have worked to deserve them.

Whichever way they paid for these things, they deserve to receive them and those who get what they never paid for are sure to return them.

It is an irresponsible living to borrow a thing and not return it after you use it.

The spirit is borrowed from God, and He desires that you return it after your roam on earth; the flesh is borrowed from the earth and you are sure you cannot take it out of this place, and so is every other temporal things of life, meant to be used for a season and left behind.

One of the best legacies a man can leave behind is helping people become who they were meant to be, not bags of gold.

It is good that business comes before pleasure and any good businessman is sure to be pleased with the outcome of his business. The business of living is not an exception.

He who works without saving is sure to go starving after the workdays.

He who overdraws of his resource of living is sure to have his little belongings sold to defray his indebtedness.

A man is never worth what he spends, but what he saves.

A man of goodness is writing his testimonial,

an agent of charity is banking in intelligence,

he who toils on the course of good is preparing to be the manager of many, and whatever a man deserves, that he shall be given by nature that makes no mistakes.

I stand in awe and watch a man who is so angry his opportunistic good is not rewarded abundantly, and I ask myself what this man would be like if all the evil he committed in the past were rewarded as abundantly as he now desires.

The present generation has witnessed the boom of lovers of the heavenly kingdom, but few bearers of the king's cross.

> *Many have refused to sleep for want of consolation, but many more will dismantle their ears for the hearing of tribulation.*

Many are yearning daily for the rain of manna from heaven, but fear to step into the storms of wilderness experience.

A God of faithful provision is not a rewarder of lassitude. Every successful candidate shall be given a crown of glory but there shall be no crown without a cross attached.

> *Those who run away from the cross of life, deny the glory of the king in the sense.*

Pains make the warrior and tribulations strengthen the mind of the hopeful. There shall not be any consolation except for the reason of the tribulations.

Whatever a man sows, that exactly shall he reap, and everyman shall indeed reap what he sows.

125

PRICE

There is a price that man must pay for all his wants, even when all his needs, nature had provided them free.

It is one thing to want whatever we feel can be of benefit to us or at least, raise our status in life, but another thing to get these things for ourselves.

Darkness will come when the sun hides its face,

the bull will charge when it sees the sign of blood, the fowls will rush at where seeds are thrown and indeed, everything has its signs and signals, even the spirits of the underworld.

Every lock has a key and every item has a price; and if you can pay the price, you can get whatever you want in life.

That you search for a thing is the first prove that it exists; that you cannot find it is simply your limitations.

For all that humanity wanted, salvation, life and protection,
they were simply scared by its symbol, the cross.

There are forces everywhere on earth, working by commands and signals. Any man can harness any force to his own gain or loss, to do good or evil.

For man to be free from death, some man had to die. For man to be free from hostility, some man had to show an extraordinary love and affection in accepting the hostile of all hostilities.

Somebody must pay for riches that other people may gain from;

and indeed there would be nothing in it to gain if someone didn't take the pains.

To deny the substitution of the Lamb of Sacrifice for the sin of the nation is to deny that it was spoken and we all come into being, or can it be denied that a man issued a command and an army went to war that millions were killed?

The world is a military zone, in which

you are fought whether you are fighting or not.

You do not need to deserve hatred before you are hated and you do not need to be guilty before you are killed.

To avoid these sorts of things, you have to fight back or at least, somebody must fight on your behalf.

You are naturally attached a thousand and one invisible warriors, harness them and seek to know which one works best for you.

Nothing is given free, every man must fight for his own salvation, every man too must organize his own protection. Nothing is given to a man free that he does not have to do anything.

If you do not fight to be a victor, you are already a victim.

There is no fence to stand.

A man forgives you today, the same man kills you tomorrow for the sins he said he had forgiven you.

There is no security in this earth except in God.

Do not stick to a man and forget yourself, no man on earth is worth that level of trust.

Whatever you want in life, be happy to pay the price and take it to yourself.

Be careful of the things that come free of charge, they might not be free anyway!

The more people want a thing the less they stick to what they have. Many people have learnt to give just to receive.

CPSIA information can be obtained
at www.ICGtesting.com
Printed in the USA
BVHW031117280319
543966BV00001B/35/P